Tudor Women:
COMMONERS AND QUEENS

Tudor Women:
COMMONERS
AND QUEENS

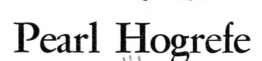

Pearl Hogrefe

THE IOWA STATE UNIVERSITY PRESS / AMES

1 9 7 5

PEARL HOGREFE is Professor of English, Iowa State University, and author of several books in her fields of creative writing and Renaissance literature. Among them are: *The Process of Creative Writing; The Sir Thomas More Circle; The Life and Times of Sir Thomas Elyot, Englishman;* and *Renewal,* a book of poems. She holds the Ph.D. degree from the University of Chicago. She has published also in the journals of her fields and, in her appointment at Iowa State, has been cited by the faculty for her creative writing activities and her outstanding and inspiring service on the staff. A major portion of her research for this book and others has been carried on at the Folger Shakespeare Library in Washington, D.C., since much information about women is in print but has not been analyzed and assembled. She did research on the background in England and also secured photostats of many important documents through friends or through correspondence with the proper officials in England.

She has had grants to aid her research: two from the Folger Shakespeare Library (1951, 1961), a fellowship from the American Association of University Women (1952–1953), two grants in recent years from the funds of the Alumni Achievement Awards, and one from Delta Kappa Gamma.

Two permanent endowment fellowships bear her name: the Pearl Hogrefe Endowment Fellowship from her former students and friends and from others who wish to support creative writing or research in literature at ISU, and the Wood-Hogrefe AAUW National Fellowship, open to competent women in any area of scholarship.

© 1975 The Iowa State University Press
Ames, Iowa 50010. All rights reserved

Composed and printed by
The Iowa State University Press

First edition, 1975

Library of Congress Cataloging in Publication Data

Hogrefe, Pearl.
    Tudor women: commoners and queens.

    Bibliography: p.
    Includes index.
    1. Women—England—Social conditions. 2. Women—England—History. I. Title.
HQ1596.H63   301.41′2′0942   75-20248
ISBN 0-8138-1695-5

CONTENTS

v

P R E F A C E

S O U R C E S for this study are varied. For the earlier centuries the economic historians, especially Ephraim Lipson with his bibliographies, have furnished many details and a general stimulus. Perhaps those of us who work in political history or the history of literature have not given the economists sufficient attention. Useful records of government, local or national, include the *Patent Rolls*, so far as they have been published, the *Letters and Papers of . . . Henry VIII*, the *Calendar of State Papers, Domestic*, as well as *Spanish* and *Foreign*, the *Calendar of Letter-Books . . . of the City of London*, and the *Reports of the Historical Manuscripts Commission*. The *STC, NED, DNB*, and the *Complete Peerage* have been indispensable; so have the *Bibliography of British History: Tudor Period*, by Conyers Read, and *Tudor England*, by Mortimer Levine. The many good or excellent full-length biographies of Tudor women—Catherine of Aragon, Queen Elizabeth, Queen Mary Tudor, Catherine Willoughby (Duchess of Suffolk), and Bess of Hardwick (Countess of Shrewsbury)—have furnished both useful background and some specific details. The two-volume work, *National Portrait Gallery Catalogue of Tudor and Jacobean Portraits* (1969) by Roy Strong, was perhaps the best reference for portraits.

Material about middle-class women is not as easily available as it is for the aristocracy or royalty. Perhaps this fact is the reason a fictional account of Anne Askew exists but only a brief, little-known biography. *Tudor Family Portrait*, by Barbara Winchester, with its valuable detail, is the record of a family, not an individual. Hence one must use faceless women or mere statistics for much middle-class background and add more detail from the landed gentry, the lesser nobility, and the aristocracy.

DETAILS OF FORM

Two classes of readers, students of history or literature in the Renaissance, and those with a taste for history (especially the history of women), but without any desire to become professional scholars, may be interested in this work. Hence efforts have been made to combine sound scholarship with simplicity of form. Author and work, when they are important sources, are often named in the discussion. For each chapter a list of sources is given, sometimes with only a general comment and sometimes with chapter or page references. Since paging in early printed books is often uncertain or inaccurate, detailed references easily become mere pedantry, especially for major ideas that are repeated throughout the book. But page references are given when they seem both accurate and useful. In the Notes, the title and the author of a book listed in the *Short-Title Catalogue* are given the original spelling, but in the discussion the spelling is modern. For a specific edition of an early book, the date is given but not the place of publication if it is London. Since some books are difficult to find, *STC* numbers are given in the Notes and Sources. Quotations in sixteenth-century spelling have been modernized, with conjectures or explanations in square brackets wherever they seem essential.

ACKNOWLEDGMENTS

Giving adequate thanks is a thorny problem arising from human fallibility about recognizing or remembering influences. The American Association of University Women contributed indirectly to this book, though many members might be surprised to learn that they have done so. In 1952 they awarded me the Founders Fellowship, giving me a year of freedom to work on another book that was later published. As my third research book comes to an end, my gratitude reaches back to what I recognize now as their act of pure faith. Two grants from the Folger Shakespeare Library, in 1951 and 1961, were of inestimable value; without them no bridge would have been built to the present. Two small grants more recently from the Alumni Achievement Fund, Iowa State University, and one from Eta chapter of Delta Kappa Gamma have also helped in completing the research for *Tudor Women: Commoners and Queens*.

Individuals have contributed. I am deeply indebted to Richard Ormond, Assistant Keeper of the National Portrait Gallery, London, for his exact, gracious, and up-to-date answers to my questions about illustrations. Many fellow readers at the Folger Shakespeare Library helped with comments or pertinent questions in informal discussions, though the details are now forgotten. Professor Albert L. Walker, Iowa State University, read early chapters and some later ones, to my profit. Mrs. Albert L. Walker and Mrs. Emerson Shideler (Mary McDermott Shideler), both experienced in research and writing and both interested in the activities of women, made valuable comments. Professor Richard L. Herrnstadt gave useful suggestions for the revision of two chapters. Elizabeth A. Windsor and Donald S. Pady, Reference Department, Iowa State University Library, have my real gratitude for putting elusive material into my hands and Linda R. Galyon, English Department, gave tireless and efficient help in reading proof. When Mrs. Carol Orr, Princeton University Press, read an early statement of my aims, her interest gave me courage about undertaking the project. Officials at Somerset House in London (while the early wills were still housed there) and at the Public Record office deserve mention for their faithful response to my requests for photostats, though I cannot thank them by name. Thomas I. Rea, Department of MSS, National Library of Scotland, Edinburgh, saw to it that a photostat of the letter Esther Inglis wrote to King James about her son's desire to study theology reached me promptly. My gratitude extends over the years to many men colleagues and a few administrators who encouraged me, granting me a tacit or a spoken equality before it became fashionable to admit women into academic life.

Four historians either raised questions or suggested valuable material: Glenn C. Nichols, once at Iowa State University, now at the University of Maryland; Marjorie Gesner, Michigan State University; Eric McDermott, S.J., Georgetown University, and Kenneth G. Madison, Iowa State University. The late Lewis M. Simes, Professor Emeritus, University of Michigan, more recently at Hastings College of Law, San Francisco, was a consultant on details of law. These professionals have saved me from errors, but they are not responsible for any that may remain.

My warm gratitude is given to Dorothy M. Mason, who exceeded the call of duty as friend and as research librarian by discussing ideas with me and by finding unusual material. She is part of a larger influence—the Folger Shakespeare Library, including the director Emeritus, Louis B. Wright; the present director, O. B. Hardison; and the friendly, efficient staff.

INTRODUCTION

T H E purpose of *Tudor Women: Commoners and Queens* is to discuss the many-sided participation of women in English life about 1485 to 1603. Thus the topic excludes characters in literature and drama and is limited to those who were once flesh and blood. Women included are those who had both the desire and the drive to achieve something individual outside the family circle, though they may also have been good wives and mothers. Nearly all classes—queens, other members of royalty, wives and daughters of peers, innumerable middle-class women—belong here. Some women of the lower classes may have had ability, but they lacked the education and the opportunity to make a recorded contribution. Women excluded are those who had wealth and position but used these assets only for personal satisfaction or led idle lives. Though the Tudor Age is the main aim, it seems necessary to lay a foundation by summarizing some activities of women before 1485, then emphasizing the activities that continued and the changes that were coming at the beginning of the sixteenth century.

One frailty of human flesh, even flesh united with a logical educated mind, it seems, is the tendency to assume, as we move backward in recorded history, that women were more fragile and sheltered. But for the Tudor period and the preceding centuries almost the reverse is true. Women like Eleanor of Aquitaine, Eleanor of Provence, Margaret of Anjou, and Cicely Neville, from the twelfth through the fifteenth centuries, did not rule in their own right, but they had executive ability, political and military skill, and a ruthlessness that at times defeated their own aims. In these same earlier centuries some women who inherited a great estate and a title when the male line failed found that they had also inherited the office of sheriff of a shire, in a few counties where the king had not yet acquired the power of appointment. Though the law permitted them to appoint a deputy, some of the women chose to perform these masculine duties themselves. In these early centuries also many women whose husbands held great landed estates guarded the properties at home or went to London as their husbands' solicitors while their men conducted a defense at home. And when the men were absent on business for the government, as they often were, the wives at home made the major decisions of both lord and lady for a complex, almost self-sustaining household and for vast farming operations. Of course they had stewards or bailiffs, with many servants, but they carried the responsibility. From peers to lower middle-class people in these centuries, a man tended to name his wife as "a whole and sole executrix" or as one of several executors when he drafted his last will and testament, and a widow often held the wardship and marriage of a son who was heir to a great estate. These vigorous women were usually spending their energy on tangible activities (though they must have learned the laws controlling their property), and they were concerned mainly with their own families.

In the same early centuries, middle-class women were active in business in many parts of England. Many managed small businesses, but a number had enterprises of considerable size. Single women and widows usually operated freely under local laws that controlled both men and women. Married women, with the consent of their husbands, might carry on businesses of their own; usually their husbands were not responsible for their business debts, and if suits connected with their businesses were decided against them, these women had to satisfy the plaintiffs themselves. Some women who carried on large enterprises were wives of wealthy London merchants. Women with small businesses were usually members of gilds, since they usually needed such a membership to do business legally; most of the early English gilds admitted women freely—maids, wives, or widows—and gave them the same privileges they granted men members.

Some of these activities of women continued through the sixteenth century. Wives of men who held great landed properties continued to make the decisions for both lord and lady when their husbands were absent, but the times were quieter; they seldom met threats of physical violence. If a small amount of evidence is representative, the women were less fearless and less vigorous. In the sixteenth century no woman seems to have become sheriff of a shire—perhaps the supply of male heirs was better—but the possibility remained. In the seventeenth century the Lady Anne Clifford inherited the office of sheriff of Westmorland and carried out some of the duties herself. Men with great estates, those with small holdings, men of all ranks and degrees in many parts of England continued to name a wife as an executrix or as one of several executors until about the middle of the seventeenth century. At that time the practice gradually dwindled away.

Two great changes came with the Tudor Age. First, few women were carrying on their own businesses after 1485 to 1500, compared with the great number that had done so earlier. Restrictive legislation was not the cause, nor is there any reason to suppose that women suddenly grew tired of working. Probably the main causes were large economic changes, fluctuations in population, and perhaps other causes not yet recognized.

The second great change, a little after 1500, was that large numbers of women were acquiring a sound classical education, with skill in speaking Latin. A few even learned to speak Greek. These women who became classical scholars were influenced by the Renaissance, by ideas of early English humanists, and especially by the theories and the practice of Sir Thomas More in educating his daughters. In a period when a thorough knowledge of Latin was necessary for a man to succeed in scholarship, in the church, or in diplomacy, a classical education for a woman was not a mere decoration. It was an aid to equality in her husband's world, a possible boon to a hostess in entertaining her husband's guests from the Continent, a means of communicating with theologians on the Continent, and a basis for making the classics and contemporary religious writings in other countries available in England. A number of women were proficient in speaking or writing French and Italian, and they used their skill in some contribution to the public good. With new ideas from the classics they enlarged their scope from tangible and physical concerns to abstract ideas on religion, education, philanthropy, and government. They ceased to be concerned only with their own landed estates and their families: they looked at England and other countries. For the first time in English history, one may say (in spite of Matilda's futile efforts to rule earlier) they became concerned with theories of government, and they ruled kingdoms in their own right.

The Tudor Age, like other periods of history, had its dichotomy. Preachers and other moralists exhorted women to be silent and obedient. Law and custom tried to enforce limitations by the use of biblical passages and the story of Eve. But many women ignored them and also the advice of the courtesy books: to be passive, gentle, and so chaste that they had not discovered physical desire. Instead they applied some of the principles recommended for Renaissance gentlemen: they developed and used all their powers. Before the time of the Tudors Christine of Pisa had observed that men trusted their wives with great business affairs and that this trust might represent life more accurately than the moralists with their accounts of Eve and the serpent. Two of her books in translation were published in England, in 1489 and 1521, and her comment applies also to sixteenth-century England.

PART ONE

Limitations on Women

CHAPTER ONE

Advice to be Passive and Subservient

T U D O R women would have been models of chaste, passive obedience if they had only followed the advice given them in much didactic literature of the sixteenth century: educational treatises, discussions on government, sermons, and other moral diatribes. Women in Continental countries during the period were apparently receiving similar advice. When Ruth Kelso, in *Doctrine for a Lady of the Renaissance,* analyzed the courtesy books for a number of countries, she concluded that the ideals for women were passive: chastity, modesty, humility, sweetness, simplicity, peaceableness, kindness, piety, temperance, beauty, sometimes learning, and always patience, charity, constancy, and obedience. She called these the Christian virtues, though Christianity includes also active virtues.

Chastity, she said, was not a requisite for men. (She might have added one outstanding exception, Elyot's *Governour,* and some of his shorter treatises written about the same time.) Chastity for women was not a mere abstinence from bodily actions: it was a purity of mind without even a consciousness of carnal desire. The qualities for Renaissance gentlemen, Miss Kelso described as classic and pagan; they were self-realization, self-expression, and a development of all one's powers. Hence they tended to be active. But the women of Tudor England made no excessive effort to remain passive, if we may judge from individual lives. Many of them, like Renaissance gentlemen, developed all their powers.

Passive qualities, recommended for the ideal woman, especially modesty and chastity, were partly an inheritance from the early fathers of the Christian church, and also from selected passages in the

3

Bible. Saint Jerome was influential; others (Clement, Cyprian, Ter-
tullian) held similar views. In a letter to Laeta about the training of
her little daughter Paula, Jerome admitted the difficulty of bringing
up children by the principles he recommended for Paula (who was to
become a nun), but he seemed to think it desirable. The mother was
to keep the girl from wanton words or acts, from knowledge of
worldly songs, from any contact with boys or with attendants who
might suggest evil, from fine clothing and jewels, paint or rouge, rich
food or much wine, and from performance on musical instruments.
Daily the girl should repeat to her mother passages from scripture,
from Greek, and later from Latin. Unless she was with her mother,
she should not appear in public, not even to visit shrines and churches.
She must learn to make wool, holding the distaff, turning the spindle,
and shaping the thread with her fingers. When she developed maturity, she must not bathe with other women or with eunuchs, but
must remain so chaste that she would blush at sight of herself.

Probably few Tudor women took with great seriousness the advice of Jerome. It is difficult to imagine vigorous, active women of
the sixteenth century blushing at the sight of their own bodies.

The few books of advice to women written before the Tudor
Age mentioned no literary training—only a strange mixture of other
qualities with passive obedience to husbands. *The Book of the Knight
of La Tour Landry* (written about 1371, so that the knight's daughters
might learn "the qualities in pure and perfect womanhood," and published by Caxton in 1484) presented the ideal of a self-regarding
woman who acted to get material rewards. She should hear many
Masses and say many prayers in order to be rewarded with a rich and
powerful knight as a husband, practice humility toward the poor to
win admiration, and learn good manners so as to be chosen as a wife
by a man of influence. Once chosen, she should be affectionate and
subservient.

How the Good Wife Taught her Daughter, a conventional
work in verse written about 1420, recommended energetic efficiency
united with some passive qualities. A wife must see that her servants
work, must work with them, and must discipline her children by beating them till they cry for mercy and admit their faults. Though it is
assumed that a woman has freedom to choose, she is advised not to
sell her handwoven cloth in the open market, not to attend wrestlings
and cockfights, not to drink too much at the tavern, and not to accept

presents from men. She must love God and attend church, speak gently, love her husband, handle him with tact when he is difficult, and obey him submissively. The work does not mention any literary education for women.

Besides the floods of discussion about the general behavior of women, two other important questions were asked in the Tudor period: Should women have a sound training in the classics, a liberal education? Should they be allowed to rule kingdoms?

The first practical defense of a sound training in the classics for women in the period was written by Thomas More, who insisted in his letter to William Gonell about 1518 that men and women were "equally suited for the knowledge of learning by which reason is cultivated . . ." His opinion, he added, was held also by "the ancients, both the wisest and the most saintly"; thus he probably had in mind the classical writers and the early fathers of the church. When William Barker wrote *The Nobility of Women* about 1559, it had become fashionable to praise women for their learning.

But by the end of the century, after a great flowering of liberal education for women, such an education was meeting with disapproval. Many parents did not wish their daughters to learn foreign languages, especially Latin. The publication of *The Necessary, Fit, and Convenient Education of a Young Gentlewoman,* written much earlier by G. M. Bruts [Bruto] but translated and issued in 1598, was one sign of the change. Though some wish to educate the girl in the humane arts and sciences, the author argued, such an education is not "convenient." Woman was given man as a companion for his labors, and thus she "ought to be attentive . . . to govern our houses." She may not take pleasure in studies "without great danger to offend the beauty and glory of her mind." Both her religious teacher and the wise matron who governs her should try to "make her humble and of a gentle and tractable spirit." Thus she would surely become a subservient wife.

When women ruled kingdoms in their own right, some men were appalled. John Knox led the crusade against them with *The First Blast of the Trumpet against the Monstrous Regiment of Women,* published in 1558 at Geneva. Filled with wrath at the execution of Latimer, Ridley, and Cranmer, he declared it "more than a monster in nature" that a woman should rule over men. Knox emphasized biblical material but also used the classics. Woman was created to serve and obey; by her fall she was doomed a second time to obedience, and she covers her head as a sign of this subjection. Saint Paul declared that she must not teach, usurp authority over men, or even speak in public meetings. Though man was made in the image of God, woman was made in the image of man. It was the duty of Christian subjects to refuse to serve under a woman and to remove her from office.

But the fiery Knox had no effect on the rule of women. Mary Tudor died before his book had time to exert an influence. Mary Queen of Scots lost the throne of Scotland because of her own conduct, not his denunciations. Queen Elizabeth merely refused him permission to enter England, and in his unbending way, he tried to make peace with her. Men who were loyal to England did not try to remove her from office because she was a woman.

Sir Thomas Smith (author of an important work, *De republica Anglorum*, secretary of state and member of the Privy Council under Elizabeth) expressed grave doubts about the rule of a woman. Though he wrote about 1565, his work was not published for about six years after his death. In Book I, Chapter 16, he granted that queens who inherited the throne had full authority; for the quiet of the realm was important, and it was understood that women rulers would have the advice of "such grave and discreet men as be able to supply all other defects." Whether Smith, like William Cecil later, changed his mind about the rule of a woman when the woman was Elizabeth, we do not know, nor do we know why he did not publish his book in his lifetime.

Men also answered John Knox, defending the rule of a woman. The best-known answer was *An Harbour for Faithful and True Subjects against the Late Blown Blast concerning the Government of Women*. It was published in Strassburg and London, in 1559. The author, John Aylmer, analyzed and refuted the arguments of Knox, calling upon the people of England to support Queen Elizabeth. John Leslie, Bishop of Ross, tried to answer Knox in 1569 (with editions in 1571 and 1584), but he emphasized the right of Mary Queen of Scots to succeed to the English throne. Richard Bertie (second husband of Catherine, Duchess of Suffolk), and Henry Howard, Earl of Northampton, wrote treatises defending a woman's right to rule, but both works remained in manuscript.

Sermons of the Tudor period, especially those preached at the celebration of marriages, often emphasized the duty of women to obey their husbands, using the story of Eve and comments from Saint Paul. The sermon Edwin Sandys (later Archbishop of York) preached during his exile, in 1559, for a wedding at Strassburg, seems typical. Though a man should honor and love his wife, he said, God gave her the law of subjection because of her transgression. Thus she should willingly and dutifully obey her husband, "else she disobeyeth that God who created woman for man's sake and hath appointed man to be woman's governor." Women, he added, should be modest in talk and dress, chaste, sober, and demure; they should stay at home instead of gadding about, and always they should obey their husbands.

Pamphleteers often sounded like preachers in their attacks on women. Geoffrey Fenton, literary man and politician, combined both classical and biblical authority in *A Form of Christian Policy*, 1574. A woman should prepare herself for humility and acknowledge that she is frail in both mind and body: "as Aristotle saith, without the guide of the man she is no other than as a matter without a form, and . . . cannot live without his direction, as being drawn out of the rib of man, and . . . was made for him, and not man for her, being the first in creation. . . ." Woman is easily carried into pride and disobedience because she is envenomed with the poison that her great mother Eve took from the serpent.

Another pamphleteer, Philip Stubbs, author of *The Anatomy of Abuses*, 1583, attacked the sins of women as if he were a preacher. He deplored the behavior of those who painted their faces, dressed their hair elaborately, wore doublets and jerkins like those of men, spent their lives in idleness and sin, and enjoyed dancing and dance music. Others expressed similar views.

Henry Smith, a famous preacher at St. Clement Danes, known as "silver-tongued Smith," gave the advice one might expect, in *A Preparative to Marriage*, in 1591. The title page states that the material was "spoken at a contract" and later enlarged. The qualities of a good wife are modesty and restrained speech, or rather, silence: "for the ornament of a woman is silence, and therefore the law was given to the man rather than to the woman, to show that he should be the teacher and she the hearer." But a husband should never chastise his wife: she is one flesh with him and he would never strike himself. She should wear sober attire, be a helper, a comfort, a chaste woman, and a good housekeeper; she should stay at home—and be obedient to her husband.

Preachers continued to emphasize the passive quality of obedience through the close of the century and later. When Robert Wilkinson preached before the king at the marriage of James, Lord Hay, to Honora Denny, he gave similar advice. A wife, he said, is like a master's mate, not the master, of a merchant ship. She must not take it upon herself, as many women do, to build churches or "to chalk out discipline" for the church. But since the wife is the weaker vessel, he exhorted the husband to use wisdom and patience with her and to love her as he loved God. If the husband must exercise his authority, it is "tempered with equality; the wife is . . . to be governed with love, not overruled by tyranny." He added that "a good wife by obeying her husband rules him."

As the study of Tudor life indicates that many women were neither passive nor subservient, a suspicion grows that they received the advice to be so, from many sources and often, because they were not heeding the admonitions. When Wilkinson told the bride that women should not build churches nor "chalk out discipline," he said, "as many women do." Those four words may be the clue to much repetition of the advice.

Writers on the law, as well as moralists and preachers, called upon the Bible to justify the obedience of the wife. The author of *The Law's Resolutions of Women's Rights*, known only as T. E., said in 1632, ". . . Eve, because she had helped to seduce her husband, hath inflicted upon her an especial bane. *In sorrow shalt thou bring forth thy children; thy desire shall be subject to thy husband, and he shall rule over thee.*"

The suspicion that women were being exhorted to obedience often because they did not heed the exhortations is somewhat confirmed by the comments of foreign visitors in the latter part of the sixteenth century. They thought that Englishwomen were active, not passive, and that they had freedom of movement, dress, and general behavior. An amusing reaction is that of Erasmus in a letter of 1499 to Fausto Andrelini. In England the lady of the house and her daughters received guests with kisses and said farewell to them with more kisses; if his friend had once tasted those fragrant greetings and farewells, Erasmus said, he would wish to travel forever in England. The same freedom of behavior was confirmed in 1585 by Samuel Kiechel, a merchant of Ulm in Suabia; he noted that a guest or a business caller who failed to kiss the hostess and the daughters was considered ill-bred or ignorant.

Samuel Van Meteren, an Antwerp merchant who lived in London and who traveled through much of England in 1575, said that Englishwomen had the free management of their houses and could go to market, to buy whatever they liked, and they were shown great honor at banquets and feasts. They had much time, he said, to walk, ride, play cards, and visit their friends—all this with the knowledge and permission of their husbands; as a result, England was known as the paradise of married women. Perhaps Van Meteren was speaking of the wealthy merchant class without intellectual interests. He added that unmarried girls were kept more strictly in England than in the Low Countries. Frederick, Duke of Wirtemberg, visiting England in 1592, reported that women had more freedom in England than in any other place. Other nations have a saying, he added, that "England is a paradise for women, a prison for servants, and a hell or purgatory for horses—for the females have great liberty and are almost like masters. . . ."

The advice that moralists and preachers gave Tudor women certainly differs from the active lives of many women in the period. When husbands trusted their wives to manage great estates in their absence or to handle the vast properties named in their wills, perhaps their confidence represents life at the time better than all the advice about being passive and obedient. Actions spoke more loudly than words. Certainly many men would have been poorer in material possessions, in the scope and enjoyment of their personal lives, and in their final fame, and England would have achieved only part of its greatness in the Renaissance if women had been passive and subservient.

The chapters that follow are concerned with the activities of those Tudor women who had the vigor and the ability to achieve something more than personal status. On every level except perhaps the lowest, where they were handicapped by poverty and ignorance, they broke through conventions and assumed responsibilities. Many of them succeeded in their endeavors.

CHAPTER TWO

Limitations by Law
and Custom

T U D O R women under public law had almost no rights. Their limitations were well established by the time of Edward I, and some of them continued even into the twentieth century. "In the camp, at the council board, on the bench, in the jury box," according to Pollock and Maitland, there was almost no place for a woman. With a few exceptions, she could not give evidence in court. In 1632, T. E., author of *The Law's Resolutions of Women's Rights,* concluded that law and divinity had shaken hands about the subjection of women. In the third section of Book I he said the cause was Eve's transgression, adding, "women have no voice in Parliament, they make no laws, they abrogate none. All of them are understood either married or to be married, and their desires or [are?] subject to their husbands. I know no remedy, though some women can shift it well enough."

In the thirteenth century probably a woman could not have inherited the throne of England. But queens had acted as regents in the absence of their husbands, as Catherine of Aragon and Catherine Parr did in the sixteenth century. When Mary Tudor came to the throne in 1553, however, she secured a declaration from Parliament that her royal power was equal to that of any king—as if doubt might exist.

But under private law an unmarried woman or a widow had almost the same rights as a man—rights that had developed by the time of Edward I. She could inherit property, at least in theory; she could hold land "even by military tenure . . . own chattels, make a will, make a contract . . . sue and be sued." If she wished, she could plead in person. If she were under a guardian, the control over her

10

was severe, but was severe also on a young man. Naming the six ages for a girl in 1641, William Noye stated she was free of wardship at sixteen; her brother, if under a guardian, waited till twenty-one to take over his property. A lady might hold the wardship for children of her tenants; a widow could become the guardian of her own children. She was not barred because she was a woman, but if she had to buy the wardship she might have stiff competition for a valuable investment.

When there was no son to inherit but more than one daughter, the daughters shared equally. But the principle of "impartible succession" affected sons and daughters alike; for in a great estate held of a feudal lord, property and office must be passed as a unit; castles or other chief dwellings belonging to barons could not be divided. Thus primogeniture developed, with the estate going to the oldest son. This principle recognized the right of the king or other overlord, not the rights of several sons. When several daughters were heirs, the seat of a baron, for example, might go to the oldest daughter, but she received a smaller amount from the remainder of the estate; and for certain feudal obligations, she or her husband represented the whole estate.

Two chief ways were developed for circumventing the right of a daughter to inherit her father's property. One was freedom of testation: by his will a man could cut off his children or any other blood relatives. In earlier centuries some limitations on this right had existed, both for personal property and for real estate, but these had become insignificant by the Tudor period. Of course a man could not dispose by will of his wife's dowry or jointure, and if property had been entailed to pass to a man's heirs, whether they were sons or daughters, he could not break the entail—at least in theory. But a father with one or more daughters and no son might will his property to his brother or his brother's son, to carry on the family name. One daughter who was disinherited by her father was Anne Clifford (1590–1676). When her father, George, Earl of Cumberland, died, he willed his estates to his brother and then to his nephew. They were to return to Anne only if the male line failed. It is said that they had been entailed from the time of Edward II to pass to the direct heir, whether son or daughter. Though Anne, her mother, and Anne's second husband filed suits to recover, Anne did not receive the estates until 1643, when the male line failed.

The other way of circumventing a daughter's right to inherit was to apply a principle developed at the common law: male heirs were preferred before female. When Catherine Willoughby's father died in 1526, she was his only direct heir and expected to receive all property not entailed to male heirs. But her father's brother, Sir Christopher Willoughby, tried to take over the estate as the next male heir. When the Duke of Suffolk bought the wardship of Catherine—and later married her—Catherine retained most of her property, but some details of the dispute, according to Evelyn Read, a biographer of Catherine, were not settled till 1564–1565.

Another daughter who had trouble inheriting was Lady Mary Cholmondeley (1563–1626). When her father, Charles Holford of Cheshire, died in 1581, his half-brother claimed all the estate as the next male heir. Lady Mary brought suits for forty years. About 1620, friends persuaded the opponents to accept equal shares; and she received Holford Manor.

When a woman married in Tudor England (and later and earlier also) her property came immediately under the control of her husband and remained under his control during the marriage. By law she was under his guardianship, becoming a feme covert, a sheltered, protected woman. All her chattels became his property. He could even claim the ownership of her wearing apparel and her jewels or other adornments. The canonists, according to Michael M. Sheehan, tried to establish her right to the chattels she had at marriage and to a share in her husband's chattels at his death, but they had little effect. Her chattels real, "such as a term of years, a wardship, a statute merchant or staple," were halfway between. Like other chattels, they became the property of the husband so that he could alienate them, that is, transfer their ownership to another person. But if he did not alienate them while he lived, they belonged to the wife at his death. He could not will them to others, and they did not pass to his nearest kin as his own chattels did.

During the marriage the husband had complete control over his wife's freehold interest in land, with no check of any kind over him. If no child was born alive of the marriage (the test being that the child was heard to cry), the wife's real estate went to her heirs at her death; but if a child had been born alive, the husband was "entitled to an estate in the whole of the wife's lands for his life." He did not lose his right if the child died immediately after it cried or if he became a widower and married again. His interest was called "tenancy by the curtesy," or "tenancy by the law of England." Historians of the law seem uncertain about the origin of his right. "Perhaps in the old days the husband may have got his right as guardian of the children," Holdsworth suggested. But someway he began to keep the right even if the child died, leaving no need for a guardian. It seems probable that circumvention in favor of the man had taken place—a gradual circumvention lost in the mists of time.

Dower for the widow was a clearly established and a well-protected right. Pollock and Maitland said: "A widow is entitled to enjoy for her life under the name of dower one-third of any land of which the husband was seised in fee at any time during the marriage." She had no share in any equitable estate. She could not be deprived of her right by any act of her husband in transferring property without her consent. If she seemed to consent, she was examined apart from her husband to determine whether her action was voluntary. By local custom a widow might receive a life interest in half her husband's lands instead of one-third, but she had to prove the local custom. She could lose her right to dower for only a few well-defined causes, a chief one being that she had left her husband and was living in adultery. She did not lose her dower if she married again.

Dower was recognized at the common law, sometimes adjusted to local custom, supported by the church, and confirmed by statutes. Though church and state agreed that the adulterous wife should be punished, the church used all possible moral pressure in defending the property rights of a woman when she separated from her husband or when a marriage was annulled. As for statutes, Parliament had provided in the reign of Edward I that a widow should receive "incontinent and without any difficulty" her share: "and for her dower shall be assigned unto her the third part of all the lands of her husband which were his during coverture, except she were endowed with less at the church door." No right of a woman in the Tudor period, it seems, was better protected than the right of a widow to her dower.

The enterprising Tudor woman might use other means of securing more of her husband's property than dower, or at a young girl's marriage, her parents or her guardian might use some of them for her advantage. These means were the assent of the father *(ex assensu patriae)*, the contract at the church door *(ad ecclesiae ostium)*, and the husband's last will and testament.

When the bridegroom was under age, a consenting father as-signed property to his son's bride, to become hers at the death of her husband. By the time of Edward III a deed was required for this kind of settlement. The contract at the church door was also an assign-ment of property to a woman before her marriage, and in early cen-turies the agreement was a part of the marriage ceremony. When the bridegroom was under age, such a contract included the assent of the father; when the bride was a mature widow, it must have been an agreement between her and her future husband. In either case, the woman was to receive the property at her husband's death. Chaucer's sly suggestion that the Wife of Bath had had five husbands at the church door seems to imply that she had a good property settlement each time.

Both the assent of the father and the contract at the church door were approved by English law, discussed by Littleton in his *Tenures* as established practice, and had the support of the church. Michael M. Sheehan said: "In England the endowment of the bride at the door of the church was incorporated in the sacramental lit-urgy." In earlier centuries only an oral contract existed; if questions came up later, they were settled by a jury of those who had attended the wedding.

In *Select Cases in the Court of King's Bench under Edward I,* G. E. Sayles gave the example of a William Heron, who had agreed with a woman named Emelina for the marriage of his son Walter to her daughter Alice. In the ceremony, when Walter said, "with the third part of the lands of my father William, I thee endow," the same William agreed. He also took an oath on the altar that he would never oppose this dower. After Alice's husband had died, she petitioned the king, who ordered the sheriff of York to collect the witnesses; they proved the case for Alice, and she received the property.

A husband's last will and testament sometimes gave a wife more property than she could get by her dower rights. A man who died young, leaving small children, might will everything he had to her, with the possible exception of gifts to charity and the church, asking her to use it for herself and the children at her discretion. Or a generous, affectionate older man (with or without subtle persua-sion from his wife), one perhaps in his second or third marriage, with his daughters well settled and with no son to inherit, might will to his wife all his property.

A poor girl, from a Cornish peasant family, Thomasine Bona-ventura, acquired property by fortunate marriages to three wealthy

London merchants—Thomas Barnaby, Henry Gall, and Sir Thomas Percival. No stepchildren and no children of Thomasine are mentioned, and Percival had been important enough to serve as lord mayor of London. When he died Thomasine became a wealthy woman. In her will, 1513, she provided Masses and other prayers for the souls of all three husbands; and her holdings made possible extensive philanthropy, both in the London area and in her native Cornwall.

Bess of Hardwick was another girl who rose in both rank and property by her marriages. Though her actions were legal and not unethical by standards of her time, her successes made her conspicuous. When she was about seven, her father died, leaving her only forty marks as a marriage portion. But she had the good fortune to join the London household of Lady Zouche. Fourteen-year-old Robert Barlow came there as a guest, lingered because of illness, and developed a desire to marry Bess. The parents were willing, and apparently a settlement with the assent of the father was arranged, allowing her all that the boy would inherit, to be her jointure. She would receive it at his death. A few weeks or months later, his illness was fatal, and after his death Bess acquired his whole inheritance of lands, woods, and lead mines.

In 1547, some fourteen years later, Bess married Sir William Cavendish, a widower about forty-two. Probably these mature people arranged a settlement at the church door; perhaps no Tudor woman in her right mind would have married him without some agreement about property. He owned abbeys, rectories, and manors; he had a position at court; and he disposed of scattered holdings to consolidate his estate in Derbyshire, the home county of his new wife. He had become a widower twice before, but when he married Bess, he had no male heirs. His will is not available, but when he died in 1557, she probably took over his property for herself and their six young children. Even her dower from Cavendish, with her property from Robert Barlow, might have amounted to a small fortune.

In 1559 Bess married another widower, Sir William St. Loe. His daughters had probably been assigned good portions and jointures at their marriages. Also he had no direct male heir. When he died, probably in 1565, his will did not mention his daughters, his resentful brother who had hoped to become his heir, or any other human being except his dear wife. He gave his soul to God, his body to the earth, and all his property to Bess, with many terms of affection.

In 1567 or 1568, Bess married her fourth husband, George

Talbot, Earl of Shrewsbury, reputed to be one of the richest men in England. He owned several manors and great castles; he held a lease from the queen on Tutbury Castle. Of course Bess became a countess. She also arranged good marriages for two of her children with two of the earl's children. Her marriage settlement must have been unusual. Few women were shrewd enough before the seventeenth century to arrange settlements giving them control over any of their property. But while Bess was a feme covert, with all her property legally under the control of her husband, she finished building and furnishing Chatsworth at great cost; she apparently claimed the ownership of 8,000 sheep; and when her parental homestead came up for sale and her husband refused to put any money into it, she bought it herself. When the earl died in 1590, after years of estrangement and bitterness, his son and heir, Gilbert Talbot, was shocked at the amount of his father's property that remained in her hands; he became her bitter enemy. Bess, the girl with only forty marks as a marriage portion, had become the wealthy Countess of Shrewsbury.

Young girls still under parental control had small chance of following emotional preferences in marriage. Parents chose suitable marriages for them and were usually able to enforce the choice. Nearly all marriages were based on material concerns—money, rank, title, or political advantages. Ambitious middle-class people, wealthy merchants, landed gentry, professional men, lesser nobility, aristocracy, and royalty—all expected material gain, with or without love and affection. The Capulets, not Romeo and Juliet, represented the standard pattern. To all "right-thinking" people, father and mother knew best. Parents were able to enforce more easily standards that all classes accepted. Material bases for marriage led young tradesmen or apprentices to rise in the world by marrying the master's daughter, or even his older widow. A grocer in London, John Wells, is used as an example by A. B. Beaven in *The Alderman of the City of London*. He married a widow with a dower of £764, was appointed guardian of her children, and secured permission to use their share of the property, an additional £764, in his business. The same bases for marriage led gentlemen of the law and other worthy gentlemen to seek out widows with property when they married.

The cold, formal relationship that existed between parents and children (with exceptions, of course) perhaps helped parents to enforce their wishes about husbands for their daughters. A child at its birth was often turned over to a wet nurse who suckled it for two or three years, with an occasional visit from the mother. Classical writers had recommended breast-feeding by the mother. Sir Thomas More said in 1516 that every mother in Utopia, unless prevented by illness or death, nursed her own child. Erasmus, in his colloquy, "The New Mother," about 1526, stressed the duty of every mother to suckle her child. Thomas Tusser, in *Housewifery,* perhaps about 1573, said that the good wife offers her breast to her children. But the advice must have fallen on barren ground; for Lawrence Stone, in *The Crisis of the Aristocracy,* said that the Earl of Northumberland, in 1596, was "one of the earliest advocates of breast-feeding." Perhaps he was—in the aristocracy. Formal relationships were furthered also because children were sent at an early age to other households for training, put into the care of a private tutor, sent to a university, or placed in a lesser Inn of Court for the study of law.

These formal relationships, with parental actions based on family pride, not affection, perhaps led mothers to beat daughters who would not consent to an arranged marriage. The most vivid account available, in *The Paston Letters,* edited by James Gairdner, happened earlier than the Tudor Age, but it suggests later possibilities. When Agnes, the widow of Judge Paston, tried to force her daughter to marry the repulsive-sounding Scrope, the girl rebelled. Her cousin, Elizabeth Clare, wrote the victim's brother on June 29: "And she has since Easter for the most part been beaten once in the week or twice, and some time twice in one day, and her head broken in two or three places." Probably Lady Jane Grey was cursed by her father and beaten by her mother because she flatly refused at first to marry Guildford Dudley. Though the detailed references given by Richard Davey, in *The Nine Days' Queen,* are unavailable, Lady Jane's comments to Roger Ascham, as he reported them in *The Schoolmaster,* offer indirect evidence. For small faults she received pinches, nips, and other punishments she would not even name because she honored her parents; sometimes she thought herself in hell when she was with them. She contrasted their treatment of her with the kindness of her tutor, John Aylmer, and his "fair allurements" to learning. Such parents would not hesitate to beat a daughter when a throne was at stake, as it was in the marriage to Guildford Dudley.

The need of a marriage portion was another factor impelling a daughter to marry the man her parents chose for her. Nearly every prospective husband was interested in its size, and without it a daughter could not hope for a desirable marriage. Often the portion was a considerable sum paid in installments. In the early part of the century when Bess of Hardwick had only forty marks, Catherine Parr and her sister had £400 each. "Between 1530 and 1570, inflation steadily raised the average figure to more like £1,000." In 1571 Lord Burghley paid a portion of £3,000 when his daughter Anne was married to the Earl of Oxford. Marriage was almost universal. A girl had no desirable alternative. Before the Dissolution she might enter a convent. But some of the more desirable religious houses required a fee, involving parental consent again; and many able-bodied daughters were reluctant to leave the secular world. Almost the only other choice was to become a dependent in the household of a relative. Hence a girl would think twice before she forfeited her portion.

Fathers often wrote wills stating that daughters would not receive portions or even funds for their maintenance until they reached the age of marriage if they refused to marry the man chosen by parents, by a guardian, or even by an executor of a will. Occasionally fathers willed daughters in marriage as if they had been chattels. Robert Burdon, a gentleman of Northamptonshire, stated in his will of 1533 the agreement he had made with a local yeoman, Roger Knollys: his oldest son was to marry the yeoman's oldest daughter "at or before the age of nineteen. If she died, he was to marry any other daughter chosen by Knollys; if he died, his place was to be taken by the second son, and if he also died, by the third." Though tolerance may have been developing in the latter part of the sixteenth century, as Lawrence Stone and Mildred Campbell both suggest, some fathers, more often those in north England, remained conservative. In 1599 William Shaftoe, in Northumberland, included this clause in his will: "To my daughter Margerie, LX sheep, and I bestow her in marriage upon Edward, son of Reynold Shaftoe."

Fathers who were aristocrats applied the same pressures about the marriage of their daughters. Lawrence Stone gives a long list, through the sixteenth century, of those who stated that the daughter's portion depended upon her willingness to marry the man chosen by her parents or her guardian. In 1581 the second Earl of Southampton ordered his executors to cut off both the portion and the maintenance fund for his daughter if she dared to disobey them.

A girl's right to choose her husband was further limited by the fact that most girls and many boys were married so young that the law did not permit marriage without the consent of parents or guardians, and when they were not mature enough to make effective resistance. Girls of royal and aristocratic families were sometimes married at fourteen or fifteen; for other girls, sixteen or later was usual. Parents sometimes had reasons for making early contracts for marriages: they wished to capture desirable marriage partners when they were available; they feared that the early death of a father, in an age of early deaths, would place the child and the estate under a guardian not chosen by the family; and Catholic parents, under Elizabeth and Lord Burghley, feared a guardian who would educate the child to a change of religion. Even though it was easier to break a contract for a marriage that had not been consummated, some parents merely drew up firm contracts for a future marriage; some took the risk of token marriages, by having a ceremony before the bridegroom left for the Continent on an educational tour; others permitted the ceremony but took their daughter home to live with them. Parents who read the popular medical treatises (Thomas Paynell's translation of *Regimen sanitatis Salerni*, 1528; Thomas Cogan, *The Haven of Health*, 1584, and similar works) were warned that early marriages might lead to stunted children, cause permanent damage or endanger the life of a girl who bore a child before she was sixteen, and an early sex life might "impair a young man's physical and intellectual development." But parents who weighed these dangers might make contracts for future marriages. And even if children were of age when they married, the girl's father had to provide a portion, and the bridegroom's father had to arrange living expenses for his son and heir and a jointure for the bride when and if she became a widow. Parents might withhold these funds and thus control the choice of their children in marriage.

A girl under a guardian might be worse off than one whose parents were living. Though a guardian could not compel a ward to marry a person he chose, he could exact a heavy fine from the estate for a refusal. If he planned to marry a ward to his own son or daughter, to enhance the prestige of his family, or if he planned to marry a girl ward himself, the young person might find it difficult to refuse. When Charles Brandon, Duke of Suffolk, bought from the king the wardship of Catherine Willoughby, a baroness with property, he perhaps meant to marry her to his son. But when his wife, Mary, the younger sister of the king, died in June, 1533, he married Catherine himself in September of the same year. He was about forty-seven and she was fourteen. She had been a member of his household for several years; and if she had wished to refuse the marriage, she would have found it difficult. By Tudor standards it was a brilliant match, making her, after royalty, the second ranking duchess in the kingdom. Whether the marriage was unhappy or happy we do not really know; but for some reason Catherine, when she became mature, practiced firm ideas about letting young people and others make their own choices. In 1550 when Edward Seymour, protector to Edward VI and at that time the most powerful man in England, wished her to join him in arranging a marriage contract between her son and his daughter, she refused to do so: they were too young to make a choice, and to choose for them would be wicked. When her son by her second marriage, Peregrine Bertie, wished to marry the sister of the Earl of Oxford, Edward Vere, she disliked the idea and tried to talk him out of it. When she failed to change his mind, she asked her friend, Lord Burghley, to help secure the queen's consent to the union.

Catherine's second marriage defied all the Tudor conventions. She married Richard Bertie, a gentleman usher in her household; he had neither wealth nor titles. But he did have wisdom, judgment, and a good education; he was a friend and advisor who apparently helped her bear the shock when both her sons by her first husband, Charles Brandon, died of the plague; and he also shared her religious beliefs.

The voice of Catherine, Duchess of Suffolk, did not cry alone in the wilderness against forced marriages. About 1548 H. Brinkelow, in *The Complaint of Roderyck Mors,* deplored sales of the marriages of wards because such sales led to adultery. In 1582 George Whetstone, in *An Heptameron of Civil Discourses,* described forced marriages as the most extreme form of bondage in existence. But in 1589 John Stockwood, author of *A Bartholomew Fairing for Parents,* attacked the tendency of young people "to follow their own will and let out the reins unto their own . . . unsettled lusts." In 1598 Robert Cleaver, in *A Godly Form of Household Government,* conceded that parents may plan contracts; but a contract, he added, is "a voluntary promise" and should be broken if the parents learn that either one of the pair has a loathing for the other. A contract based on force, violence, or dissimulation is not voluntary. Though Puritans stressed obedience to parents, they disliked contracts with only a material basis and believed affection to be the foundation of stability in the family. In the early seventeenth century playwrights began to develop the theme of choice in marriage. In 1607 *The Miseries of Enforced Marriage,* by George Wilkins, and about the same time *The Yorkshire Tragedy* were based on this idea. Both plays, it is said, were evolved from an actual tragedy, the Calverley murders, resulting from an arranged marriage.

A young girl who was accepted as a maid of honor at the court had no right to marry without the royal permission. In accepting her, the queen assumed for her the role of a parent, and both the girl and her own parents hoped that she would make a good or even a brilliant marriage. In that select men's club (as Sir John Neale called the court of Elizabeth) she might marry beneath her or become the victim of an unscrupulous courtier. So the queen punished the guilty ones who were discovered. When Elizabeth Throckmorton became pregnant by Sir Walter Raleigh, they pleaded that they had planned to marry, but the queen sent them as prisoners to the Tower. But though the queen needed to be strict and to punish offenders at times, her theories of ruling included an attractive court, with beautiful girls and unmarried courtiers. And though an older Elizabeth may at times have envied a pretty young girl, her actions, perhaps, were not based upon jealousy as much as some writers imagine. Instead they were based upon a real need for discipline.

When a young girl was both a maid of honor and a person of royal blood with some claim to the throne, her marriage without the royal blessing was treason. But with her dislike of bloodshed, Elizabeth sent the guilty ones to prison, not to execution. When she punished the younger sisters of Lady Jane Grey for their secret marriages, probably her motive was not feminine jealousy. They were granddaughters of Mary, the younger sister of Henry VIII; since he and Edward VI had both named the descendants of the Suffolk line as next in succession after Henry's own daughters, their marriages involved political considerations.

Young girls who were the daughters or the sisters of rulers were doubly handicapped about the choice of a husband since royal marriages were usually political alliances. Henry VIII, for example, used his daughter Mary as a political pawn: she was formally betrothed to the little dauphin when she was two years old, and to Charles V, King of Spain and Emperor, when she was five. Her father used her in a different kind of political game when he forced her religious submission to keep his enemies from basing a rebellion on her as a loyal Catholic. When she became queen at thirty-eight years of age, she chose Philip II of Spain as her husband; but though she gave him complete devotion, he had married her only to gain political power.

When Elizabeth became queen, political realities, not a brother or a father, kept her from marriage. She could not choose a subject without creating more bitter divisions in England, and she did not dare to marry Leicester, the one subject she might have chosen, after the strange death of his wife, for she would have lost her reputation and her power over her people. She could not marry a foreign prince, Protestant or Catholic, without a loss of power. And she had a consuming ambition to be a great queen.

Women in the Tudor Age did not often acquire rank or title through their own achievements but only through their fathers and their husbands. But Henry VIII granted property and the title, Marchioness of Pembroke, to Anne Boleyn before he was legally free to marry her—probably the price of her physical surrender. A few other women, before and after the Tudors, were given titles directly by rulers.

Some women, eager for titles, used them without any right to do so. Though London aldermen had no titles, their wives sometimes insisted on being called *Lady*. The widow of a knight, according to William Harrison, might continue to be called *Lady*, but by courtesy only: "she pretendeth to lose no honor through courtesy yielded to her sex; she will be named after the most honorable or worshipful or both, which is not seen elsewhere." The lowborn wife of a nobleman kept his rank and title when he died unless she had returned to her father with her dowry or was married again. If she married a second time and the husband was a nobleman, she acquired nobility through him. Especially in cases of high rank she might continue to be called by her former title as a courtesy. For example, Mary, the sister of Henry VIII, after Louis XII had died and she had married the Duke of Suffolk, continued to be called the French queen, informally; and Catherine, Duchess of Suffolk, continued to be called the duchess after she had become a dowager and even after she had married Richard Bertie. But a woman who had inherited a title, according to Edward Chamberlayne and others, had the clear right to retain that title for her life.

A woman had the right to transmit to her son titles she had inherited but not to her husband. Catherine Willoughby, baroness by inheritance, tried to persuade the queen to give Richard Bertie the title "Baron Willoughby" after she had married him. Though commissioners examined the problem and her good friend, William Cecil, tried to help her, the queen did not respond. But later she bestowed the title on their son, Peregrine Bertie.

Women had a right to the protection of person and property, and the statutes of Parliament record a continued effort to prevent their abduction. Perhaps men were really protecting themselves by these laws, for nearly every woman with property would become a wife, with her property under the control of her husband. The preamble of a law passed about 1453 stated that men of great covetousness were trying to get into their power "ladies, gentlewomen, and other women sole" who had property. Using dissimulation or force, they would take the women to the part of the country where they—the abductors—had the greatest power. Then they would try to bind the women to obligations about their property or to force them into marriage. The statute gave the woman the right to sue a writ compelling the chancellor to summon the offender, examine the case, and give justice. But if a woman was a prisoner in a strong castle, she could sue a writ out of chancery in theory only; and if she had been pressured into marriage or was the victim of physical atrocities, the writ might not be a complete remedy.

Abductions continued. A similar statute was passed in the third year of Henry VII, another under Queen Mary about 1557, and another under Elizabeth in 1597. The last of them began with the statement that maids, wives, and widows with property were still being abducted and defiled or forced into marriage. In future, an offender would lose all right to benefit of clergy and would be condemned to death.

One must conclude, then, that public law gave Tudor women almost no rights, and that all their property—lands, houses, even personal clothing, jewels, and other adornments—came under the complete control of their husbands. But private law gave single women or widows almost the same rights as men, but these rights could be circumvented. Also young girls had little chance to choose their own husbands. One must conclude also that dower rights for widows were well defined and well enforced, and that a widow with property had much freedom. She could manage her own property and, with the exception of her dower, dispose of it by will; she could choose a second husband, or a third or a fourth; she could handle a marriage settlement with the proper retreat or advance, according to her skill in persuasion or the ardor of her suitor.

But Tudor society was patriarchal. To recite the controls over women only would distort truth. Primogeniture was an injustice to younger sons. In families of the aristocracy they might be given small annuities or a life interest in a small estate, or they might become stewards for family properties. They could not seek employment outside the family; they could seldom finance desirable marriages. In families of yeomen, younger sons were sometimes treated in the same way.

In such a patriarchal society, the heir to an estate also had his problems. He had to depend on his father to provide an income for him and his bride during his father's life and a jointure for his bride when and if she became a widow. Without these two financial arrangements, marriage for him was practically impossible. Hence father held the whip hand about the choice of his son's bride and the time of the marriage. When Sir Walter Mildmay, for example, made plans for his son Anthony to marry Grace Sherrington, the son hesitated, not because he disliked Grace, but because he wished first to see something of the world. If the son refused to marry her, the father said, he would not help him to any marriage in the future. So he married Grace, but he left her with his parents while he used most of their living allowance in seeing the world. Like his sister, or his sisters, then, the son and heir might be compelled to let his father choose the time of his marriage and the girl who would become his wife.

But in spite of restrictions many Tudor women managed to act with considerable freedom. They held unusual positions, carried on large businesses of their own, managed great estates in the absence of their husbands, executed last wills and testaments, earned a sound classical education, promoted their religious views, aided in the development of literature, and sometimes arranged marriage settlements to increase their future property beyond the dower, or managed to keep control over the property they already owned. As T. E. said nearly a generation after the Tudors, "some women can shift it well enough."

PART TWO

 Escape from Limitations in Action

CHAPTER THREE

Women Officeholders

I N the Tudor Age, and also in earlier centuries, women sometimes held positions of great responsibility, either by election, by inheritance, or by informal or formal appointment. They were elected as churchwardens; in the absence of a male heir, they might inherit a great estate and a title along with the office of sheriff for a whole shire or county; they were often named by their husbands in wills as the "sole and only executrix," or as one of several executors for great estates. Probably the Lady Margaret Beaufort was named by her son, Henry VII, as High Commissioner of the Council of the North.

A woman who served as a churchwarden was elected to the office, and it seems apparent that she must have had business acumen and executive ability. As early as the thirteenth century these wardens were chosen annually in a parish meeting presided over by the rector or vicar, with all the adult members voting. Usually two wardens served together, now and then one seems to have served alone, and sometimes additional ones were elected for special or unusually heavy duties. J. C. Cox and F. A. Gasquet listed a few women wardens before the time of the Tudors, but most of those they mention served after the accession of Henry VII. The earliest women that either author names as wardens were Alice Cooke and Alice Pyppedon, joint wardens at St. Patrick, Ingestre, Staffordshire, in 1426–1427; and Beatrice Bray at St. Petrock's, Exeter, in 1428. Within the Tudor period, Dame Isabel Norton (or Newton?) was elected as a warden in Yalton, Somersetshire, in 1496. Luce Sealy seems to have served alone at Morebath, Devonshire, in 1548. And a woman was one of the churchwardens at Kilmington, Devonshire, in 1560, 1569, 1570, 1574, 1578, and 1581.

The responsibilities of churchwardens seem overwhelming. The possessions of a parish included lands, houses, flocks, herds, and even hives of bees, with gifts being added all the time. As a result, wardens had to oversee farming operations, buy and sell produce, or dispose of gifts to the best advantage. They arranged for building, repairing, or decorating both the church and the common house. They saw that money due to the common purse was paid, devised some way of raising funds or doing any extra work the parish had undertaken, planned church ales, women's feasts, and hockdays (usually festivals for raising money by humorous methods), attended visitations, and arranged with the bishops and found fees if a church, a cemetery, or a new chalice had to be consecrated. They were the guardians of jewels, plate, ornaments, hangings, tapestries, and vestments. When the church needed a new peal of bells, repairs on the organ, or new plate, the churchwardens carried out the decisions of the parish. They also presented to the archdeacon's court parishioners who had been guilty of immoral conduct. Sometimes they were the guardians of a common chest from which parishioners might borrow funds to help them through times of misfortune. Thus their work included the management of farming and livestock, selling produce, supervising repairs, buying materials and objects for the church—as well as duties rising from hard luck and from sin.

For these many-sided responsibilities, women who served must have received both thanks and complaints but no tangible rewards, nothing except the consciousness of duties well performed, no increase in their personal rights, but only a chance to use their abilities.

Women were given heavy responsibilities when they were named as the chief persons or the only persons to execute the last wills of their husbands or of other members of their families. They were often named for this duty before and during the Tudor Age, in all parts of England and in all classes of society. Perhaps it is not surprising that they were selected when they managed manors in the absence of their husbands, or in earlier periods, when women like Isabel (the wife of James Berkeley) or Margaret Paston persuaded justices of the peace that their husbands were in the right, pleaded for their husbands in court, or defended manors. A woman like Catherine, Duchess of Suffolk, named first in the list of the executors for the duke's great estates (when he died in 1545) and given the wardship and marriage of their son and heir, carried enormous responsibilities.

The statement that women were often appointed to execute

the wills of their husbands, before and through the sixteenth century and for a generation or so after, is based on wills examined in Bedfordshire, Berkshire, Lancaster, Cheshire, Durham, Bury St. Edmunds, Stratford-on-Avon, and other parts of England. In these wills a woman was called an executrix when she was named alone, but when she was appointed with one or more men, all were called executors. For example, Richard Hathaway of Stratford, after naming other bequests, left the remainder of his goods to "Joan, my wife, whom I make my sole executrix. . . ." And Roger Sadler, of the same place, left all unbequeathed property to "Margaret, my loving wife, and my cousin, Hamnett Sadler, whom I do also make and ordain to be my executors of this my last will and testament." In modern usage (except for some legal documents) an executor is a *person,* not exclusively a man. In this discussion, then, the term executor or executors will be used for men or women.

Among the many men who trusted their wives to execute their wills was William de Pole, in 1448: "And I ordain my best-beloved wife my sole executrix. . . ." If she wished, he added, she might choose a person "to labor under her as she would command him." Henry VII, in 1509, named his "most entirely beloved mother, Margaret, Countess of Richmond," first among his executors. In 1505 Sir Henry Colet, twice mayor of London, selected his wife, Dame Christian, and his son, John Colet. In 1519 the same John Colet, Dean of St. Paul's, named his mother, and two men with her; though Dame Christian had reached a great age by this time, she was unusually alert. The families connected with Sir Thomas Elyot often named women, the favorite being Elyot's stepsister, Dame Susan Kingston. About 1514 her husband, John, left her all his property and the disposition of a considerable estate. About 1526 her grandmother, Dame Alice Bessils, chose her as one of her executors; and in 1529 her uncle, William Fettiplace, included her and his sister, Dame Marie Englefield, as two of his seven executors.

In 1545 Charles Brandon, Duke of Suffolk, named first his wife, Catherine. He added as other executors the Lord Chancellor Wriothesley, Sir Anthony Browne, and William St. John, who was lord chamberlain of the king's household. Then he humbly asked the king himself to act as overseer. William Tallis, the musician, dying about 1585, appointed his wife Joan as his sole "executrix," but named as overseers William Byrd, the musician (who had been his student), and also Richard Cranwell. In 1586 Sir Philip Sidney named his "most dear and loving wife, Dame Frances Sidney" as his sole "executrix," leaving her half his property holdings for her life and all other unbequeathed property, including chattels. He named five supervisors also—the Earls of Leicester, Huntingdon, Warwick, and Pembroke, and his wife's father, Sir Francis Walsingham. In 1590 Walsingham named his wife, Dame Ursula, as his "trustie sole and faithful executor." In 1592 Arthur Dakins of Hackness, Yorkshire, named only his wife and his daughters.

Shakespeare's contemporaries in Stratford furnish many examples of women executors, mostly from the wills of middle-class people. In his first volume of *Testamentary Papers: Wills from Shakespeare's Town and Time,* E. Vine Hall reproduced nine wills. Five of them designated the wife, three of them emphasizing that she was the only one to administer the will; one named her son with her, and the fifth named the wife without comment. Two of the five testators identified themselves as bakers, one as an ironmonger, and one as a gentleman. Of the other four wills, one testator was a widow, one a widower with five children, and two were men who did not mention a wife or children but left money to a mother and brothers.

Hall's second volume contains ten wills of Stratford people, from 1578 to 1603. Two of the wills were made by widows. Two selected the wife but added a male relative as a second executor; one left bequests to a wife but named a son-in-law as the only executor. The other five testators designated the wife as "sole" or "whole and sole" person to handle the estate.

Dozens of such examples could be found, but these seem representative. Of course the wife could be effective only when she had full knowledge of her husband's financial affairs. In commenting on the decline of the practice, Alice Clark said that naming the wife continued to be the usual practice even in the first half of the seventeenth century. By the Restoration, a change came because "The winding up of a complicated estate could not have been successfully undertaken by persons who hitherto had led lives of idleness, unacquainted with the direction of affairs."

But though women were commonly given the complex responsibilities of executing the wills of their husbands, even for the greatest estates, they did not have the clear, unrestricted right to make wills unless they were single or had become widows. At the common law it was assumed that married women could make wills only if their husbands consented. But local custom sometimes upheld their right, and the church or the canonists tried to give them support. In discussing the views of the canonists, Michael M. Sheehan stated that all adults should be permitted to make bequests, and that a desire to give alms and to manifest affection by bequests was superior to any laws made by men. Here and there, in the fourteenth and fifteenth centuries, the wills of married women were probated; about 1347–1348, in the diocese of Rochester, a number of husbands presented for probate the wills of their wives.

In the sixteenth century the inability of married women to make wills was given a renewed emphasis. Parliament in 1544 enacted this statute: "Wills or testaments made of manors, tenaments, or other hereditaments, by any woman covert, by a person under twenty-one, by an idiot, or by any person not sane, shall not be good under law." About this time also, according to Michael M. Sheehan, men were extending their control over movable or personal property and denying the right of a wife to make it the subject of a bequest. By the reign of Elizabeth the claim of the wife was declared invalid. Thus the common law was prevailing over the ideas of the canonists, and the rights of women were decreasing.

The statute of 1544, however, did not keep Anne, the first wife of Francis Walsingham, from making a will in 1564, apparently with the approval of her husband, and including both personal belongings and lands. Anne was the daughter of Sir George Barnes (lord mayor of London, 1552), the widow of Alexander Carleill, and the owner of much property when she married Walsingham. As she had no children by him, he had no "curtesy" right in her lands. A main purpose of her will was to arrange for the education, other expenses, and inheritance of Christopher, her son by her first marriage. In the will she left money to several brothers, a diamond to one brother, and personal belongings to other people; she willed to her husband, Francis Walsingham, a hundred pounds "of lawful money of England," and named him as executor. Concerning her son, she said:

I will that my said husband shall have the custody and tuition of my son . . . with his exhibition and finding during his minority and nonage . . . praying him that he will see him virtuously brought up in learning and knowledge during his said nonage. And I will that my said husband shall yield to my said son at his full age of xxi years a true and just account of all my said son's lands and movable goods during his minority.

A woman who inherited a great property and a title might discover also that she was sheriff of an English shire in a few counties where the office was hereditary, not appointive, with the sheriff named by the king. Though no woman seems to have been a sheriff in the Tudor period, the possibility continued to exist, in Westmorland and perhaps in a few other shires; but where the office was inherited, perhaps a male heir was available. Women did inherit the office in the thirteenth, fourteenth, and fifteenth centuries; and one woman, Lady Anne Clifford, was a sheriff in the seventeenth century. When a woman inherited the office, she might choose to appoint a deputy or to act in person. In the period following the Norman Conquest, the sheriff was the leader of the military forces and handled all the money collected for the king; he was an executive officer under the king and the real ruler of his shire. Though his duties had been decreasing, he still had important work in the sixteenth century: he reported the results of elections, he was responsible for making public all proclamations of the king or queen, and he had important duties at quarter sessions.

A number of women became sheriffs in the early centuries. In 1216 Lady Nicola de Haya, sheriff of Lincolnshire, appointed two men as her deputies instead of acting in person; in 1236 Ela, Countess of Salisbury, was sheriff of Wiltshire, and performed the duties in person; in 1301–1309 Margaret, widow of Edmund, Earl of Cornwall, was sheriff of Rutland, also performing the duties in person; but when she held the office another six years, she appointed three men, each in turn, to be her deputy. In 1317 Hugh de Audele and his wife were sheriffs of Rutland and may have functioned for several years in person, but seven deputies, appointed from time to time, probably did the work from 1327 to 1341. In 1449 Cicely, Duchess of Warwick, became sheriff of Worcestershire but appointed a deputy. In the reign of Edward I (if one accepts the details given by George C. Williamson, a biographer of Lady Anne Clifford) Isabella, widow of Roger de Clifford, inherited and "sat in person as sheriff" of Westmorland; a contest between Isabella and her sister Idonea about the right to the office was settled by one sister selecting a deputy and the other approving the selection. But the official list of sheriffs merely names Idonea de Leyburne along with Roger de Clifford, for 1298–1299, with a footnote adding that the king, as guardian of Isabella, assumed the right of appointment for her.

In the early seventeenth century, Lady Anne Clifford should have become sheriff of Westmorland when her father, the Earl of Cumberland, died in 1605. But since her father willed his property to male heirs (perhaps in spite of an entail) she did not win the right to possession until 1643, and because of unsettled conditions, could not return north for another five or six years. Williamson said that she employed a deputy for five years. The official list of sheriffs says only that she began to serve as sheriff January 23, 1650. She entertained the justices of the peace when they came four times a year for quarter sessions, her biographer says, and she rode to meet them, "sometimes on a white charger"; also she signed all writs certifying the election of candidates to Parliament up to the year of her death, in 1676. The Cliffords held the hereditary right to be sheriff of Westmorland up to 1850, when the family yielded so that the office might be handled as it was in the other shires of England. But the principle that a woman could inherit the office of sheriff of a shire remained valid through the Tudor period.

During the reign of Henry VII and also that of Queen Mary, some women carried great responsibilities because they were appointed to offices, and there was also much debate about their right to such appointments. In the early years of the reign of Henry VII, lawyers who worked with the king and his mother, Margaret, Countess of Richmond, supported the view that women had the right to be appointed justices of the peace. These lawyers included Thomas Marowe, Humphrey Coningsby, Robert Brudenell, and Edmund Dudley. The wording of the statutes gave some basis for their affirmative arguments. A statute enacted in the eighteenth year of the reign of Edward III provided that two or three "of the best of reputation in the counties shall be assigned Keepers of the Peace by the king's commission." And a statute in the thirty-fourth year of the reign of the same king provided that in every county "one lord and with him three or four of the most worthy in the county, with some learned in the law" shall be appointed justices of the peace. The latter statute is the basis of the system as it existed for generations, and neither law, except for the mention of one lord, specifies the sex. In the first statute, the French words are *des mieultz vauetz*, and in the second, *des meultz vauez*. Law books published about 1484 to 1504 sometimes said *men* and sometimes *persons*.

Speaking about 1503, Thomas Marowe, a serjeant-at-law, was not aware of any barrier against women, according to Bertha H. Putnam; to him the French *gentz* or *persones* meant simply human beings, and of course a woman, either single or married, could be made a justice of the peace by a commission. Marowe named Lady Nicola de Haya as one who had been a sheriff, arguing that other women could be appointed gaoleresses or sheriffs. Coningsby, in a Lent reading at the Inner Temple about 1495, supported the proposition that under certain circumstances widows might appoint justices of the peace. Brudenell insisted, apparently in a reading at one of the Inns of Court, that a woman, but not a monk, could be appointed as a bailiff. Edmund Dudley argued at Gray's Inn that the king could appoint as justices in eyre, two men either trained or untrained in the law, two aliens, or two women, either married or single.

Though these lawyers were discussing theories, possibly a few women were appointed justices about this time. It is said that the Countess of Shrewsbury was a justice of the peace in the time of Henry VII, and there is some indication of a few others during his reign. Perhaps a Lady Bartlet was a justice in the reign of Queen Mary. The evidence was mentioned in a reading on the forest law, at Lincoln's Inn, August, 1632. In that discussion, one judge said he had heard from his mother that a Lady Bartlet was a justice in Gloucestershire and "did usually sit on the bench with the other justices . . . that she was made so by Queen Mary upon her complaint . . . of the injuries she sustained by some of that county; and . . . as she herself [the queen] was chief justice of all England, so this lady might be in her own county—which accordingly the queen granted."

 In the latter half of the sixteenth century, such lawyers as William Lambarde and Richard Crompton did not mention the appointment of women. Queen Elizabeth, judging from available evidence, did not concern herself about other women in political positions of responsibility. Without the concern of a ruler and without women eager to take such positions, the whole question seems to have been forgotten for a time.

If Margaret Beaufort, Countess of Richmond, and beloved mother of Henry VII, was appointed by her son to the unusual position of High Commissioner of the Council of the North in 1507, she held the position until his death in 1509. Rachel R. Reid, in suggesting the possibility, said there is no record of any appointment for the two years, and the lack might mean that the appointment was unusual. Miss Reid also argued convincingly that the cautious Henry VII would not have left the office vacant because to do so would have been dangerous. The area had been hard to control for geographical and political reasons: great unpopulated and wooded uplands separated valleys with a few inhabitants; three noblemen held most of the land and, if united, the three could defy the king. Henry VII had met resistance when he came to the throne, and had appointed capable men, who are named, up to 1507.

Further indirect support for the idea that the Lady Margaret had held some unusual position was given by outstanding lawyers in their readings at Inns of Court in the seventeenth century. Rachel R. Reid, author of *The King's Council in the North* reported in detail on a reading by William Noye (author of law books and attorney general from 1631). In 1632, at his reading on the forest law at Lincoln's Inn, someone asked if a woman could be a justice of the forest. The question led Noye to say that Margaret Beaufort had been a justice of the peace; he had searched in vain for the commission naming her, though he had found many records of her judgments. It was not enrolled, Miss Putnam like Miss Reid suggests, because it was unusual.

Robert Callis, serjeant-at-law, commissioner of sewers for Lincolnshire, and author of *Reading upon the Statute . . . of Sewers,* also had a comment on the Lady Margaret. His material, though first published in 1647, was used in a discussion at Gray's Inn in 1622. Defending the right of women to be appointed to various commissions, he cited God's order to Adam and Eve, "the first commission ever granted"; it was in the plural, directed to both of them. Since it was customary to appoint women as executors of great estates and as guardians of minor children who would inherit immense property, he concluded that for certain positions women "have been secluded as unfit, yet they are not in law to be excluded as uncapable." After mentioning other precedents, he said, "And the wise and renowned lady, Margaret, Countess of Richmond, was put in the commission. . . ." He concluded it was warrantable to name the Countess of Warwick on the commission of the sewers. But Callis never told us what commission the Lady Margaret was given.

Lady Margaret's appointment as High Commissioner is made more probable by the fact that she had large property holdings in north England, that she and her son liked to use competent middle-class men on commissions, and that he would have had ample chance to use such men, with her as royalty at the head of the Council. No other appointment, it seems, could have done as much to break the power of the feudal lords in the north. Also, from what we know of their total relationship, the king and his mother would have agreed on the members of her Council and on other details. Of course the plan would give more power to the king—as the statutes adopted in

the reign of Edward III for justices of the peace named by him or recommended to him by his trusted advisors would give him more power. And whatever gave the king more power would decrease the power of local officials or of feudal lords.

Direct and positive evidence also exists for the assumption that Margaret Beaufort was High Commissioner for the Council of the North. In 1529 Thomas, Lord Darcy (1467–1537) prepared a petition opposing the commission that Henry VIII had given to his natural son, Henry Fitzroy, Duke of Richmond. In 1525 the king had made him the nominal head of the Council of the North, with competent middle-class men to do the work of that body; about the same time he named Princess Mary as nominal head of the Council of Wales and the Marches. On the outer leaf of his petition Lord Darcy wrote: "Memo, how the like commission that my lady the king's grandam had, was tried and approved, greatly to the king's disadvantage, in stopping of many the lawful processes and course of his laws at Westminster Hall . . . and none gain commonly by any such commission but the clerks. . . ."

Lord Darcy had every chance to know the facts when he mentioned "the like commission" given to the grandmother of Henry VIII. He was not only a contemporary but also a northern man himself, with his family seat at Templehurst, Yorkshire. So his comment may be sound. If the Lady Margaret Beaufort held this commission, and the evidence seems reasonably convincing, hers was probably the most unusual appointment given to a woman in the Tudor Age. Though Catherine of Aragon and Catherine Parr served as regents when the king was in France, precedents existed for their appointments. But the High Commissioner of the Council of the North seems to have been for all practical purposes, a vice-ruler for the troublesome shires of north England.

Women in Business: Large Affairs

A G A I N it seems necessary to say something about women in business before Henry VII came to the throne of England, as a basis for explaining what women were doing in the Tudor Age. In the thirteenth and fourteenth centuries many women carried on large business undertakings in London, trading within England or with cities on the Continent. Some of them were widows, but many seem to have been the wives of successful businessmen who became aldermen or lord mayors of London. Either the women enjoyed making additional money or they needed an outlet for surplus energy.

Margery Russell of Coventry was one of the women who carried on a large-scale business with the Continent. In 1413 when we meet Margery, London was perhaps the center of her activities, and she was a widow. She filed a declaration that she had been robbed of merchandise worth £800 by men of Santander, Spain. She was applying for letters of marque and reprisal, giving her the right to seize property from other Spaniards and thus to recover her losses. Such letters were frequent at the time; they were usually signed by the kings or by other officials of the two countries.

Margery pressed her claim successfully; for two Spaniards, it is said, appealed for the restoration of property because she or her agent had taken too much. In the list of Early Chancery Proceedings we find that "Peter Gunsales, master of the Spanish balinger, Seint Croce," had directed a writ against John Haule of Dartmouth, Devon, asking for the restitution of his balinger (a small seagoing vessel without a forecastle, much used in the period) and also his wines. His writ stated that they had been taken "under a marque granted to Margery de Coventre against the goods and men of Santander"; and according to one account, it was granted by the kings of England and

Spain. Probably Gunsales was the Spaniard who said also that he had been granted an order from the Exchequer requiring her to return part of the property. Perhaps he had encountered her before, for he predicted that she would not obey the order. Since the lists of suits in Chancery do not record decisions, we may never know how much of his property Peter Gunsales recovered. But we may conclude that Margery was a vigorous, successful woman, without overdeveloped scruples about the rights of other merchants.

A few years earlier, Richard Pafford and his wife Agnes sued for a writ in Chancery against William Nicholl and Thomas Frelond, the former mayor and the bailiff of Southampton, because they had not allowed Robert Borecroft to depart with a letter of marque, granted by Henry IV of England and by the Duke of Britanny to the said Agnes, "to recover 600 crowns against the goods of Bretons." It seems clear that the letter of marque had been granted to Agnes and that she was conducting her own business, but since she had a husband living, the law required her to name him also when she brought suit, even about her own business. Again we do not learn the result of her suit nor the reasons why the officials of Southampton detained the letters of marque, though one might guess that the Bretons had crossed their palms with silver.

Many other women in the London area were involved early in Continental trade, according to the *Calendar of Letter-Books . . . of the City of London.* The second volume, B, has more than thirty items indicating that women were handling large sums of money in businesses of their own. Leticia, the wife of Thomas le Woder, for example, admitted in the presence of two aldermen in 1312 that she owed John le Woder sixty pounds, promised to pay it in 1314, and did so. Soon she acknowledged another debt of sixty pounds and paid it. Other sources also gave details about women in business, including those cited by Alice Clark from unpublished material given her by Eileen Power. One of them, Rose de Burford, about 1318, was a large-scale trader both before and after the death of her husband, who was himself a wealthy London merchant. She was lending money to the bishop of London, and at one time she sold a cope embroidered with coral for a hundred marks. Having petitioned without success for the repayment of a loan her husband had made for the wars against Scotland, she asked permission to take the amount from the sums she paid when she shipped wool from the port of London. At some time in his reign Henry VII granted Margaret Cokkes, a widow in Calais, the right to ship from London to Southampton forty-one sacks of wool and five hundred skins with the wool still on them.

As most of the businesswomen mentioned above are recorded in the *Letter-Books . . . of London,* it is interesting to note that Volume L (the last in the series, dealing with the period from the accession of Edward IV through the reign of Henry VII) has almost no mention of women who paid or collected large sums of money. Most of the women named in Volume L were receiving property from their husbands, or they were daughters for whom property was being bonded until they should come of age or marry. Possible causes of this change were the improvement in economic conditions, the growing wealth of the merchant class, and the tendency of more prosperous merchants to buy manor houses and become landed gentry. Further attempts to give reasons for the change will be a part of the next chapter.

An Englishwoman, under the law, was either a feme covert or a feme sole. A married woman was a feme covert—a sheltered or a protected woman, under the guardianship of her husband. An unmarried woman or a widow was a feme sole. In many cities local law or custom permitted a married woman who wished to establish a business of her own to declare herself a feme sole (with the consent of her husband) only for the purposes of her business. In London her right to do so was well established. The plan was available in Lincoln and Torksey, Lincolnshire; in Hastings and Winchelsea, Sussex; in Worcester; and in Fordwich, Kent, according to Mary Bateson, in *Borough Customs.* Probably it existed in many other places also. In some localities a married woman who operated a business as a feme sole had to answer and plead like any single woman when a complaint was lodged against her; her husband was not responsible for debts connected with her business, and thus his goods and chattels could not be attached. But if she were the plaintiff in any suit, even about her separate business, she had to name her husband also, and it was the custom to name him first. About 1480, in Lincoln, if a married woman carried on her separate business while her husband was living, she was charged as a feme sole in anything that pertained to the business. If she were pronounced guilty in any suit brought against her, she was condemned to prison until she and the plaintiff came to an agreement. Mrs. Green, in her chapter on the "Town Market," makes the general statement, as if it applies to all incorporated towns, that married women could "become merchants . . . carry on a trade, hold property, and answer in all matters of business before the law as independent traders." No evidence appears to indicate that local laws or customs permitting the married woman to operate as if she were a feme sole were repealed, but as the sixteenth century advanced, it seems that few women made use of the opportunity. Late in the reign of Henry VIII, Margaret Corydon, wife of William, was admitted as a sole merchant, *ex assensu viri*, according to an item in the London City Repertories. Hence the possibility still existed at that time, though the practice seemed to be declining.

Kings used the term feme sole in giving their queens the right to manage their own properties. And Henry VII gave his mother, Margaret Beaufort, through an act of Parliament, the management of vast properties as if she were a widow, though her third husband, Thomas, Lord Stanley, was still living. He also gave his wife the same right, but with fewer and less affectionate words.

Meantime the efficient woman who handled a large business did not disappear in the sixteenth century, even if the numbers decreased. Barbara Winchester, author of *Tudor Family Portrait,* gives details of several businesswomen associated with the Johnson brothers. They seem usually to have been widows and were Englishwomen working mainly on the Continent but keeping connections with England. As Otwell Johnson died in 1551, and the firm (including John Johnson and Sir Anthony Cave) was dissolved in 1553, these women were active in the 1540's and the early 1550's.

One of the women, Jane Rawe, who may have been unmarried or a widow (probably the latter) and whom Otwell Johnson referred to as the "Hazebrouck woman," had a successful private exchange business. Her Flemish center was at Hazebrouck; and from there she traveled at need to Antwerp, Calais, and London. Another was the widow of Thomas Rose, described as a wealthy man. For a time she carried on her husband's business as a fellmonger—a dealer in hides, probably most of them sheepskins. Evidently she tired of the business or of the single life, for she soon married a Mr. Purvey, a butcher and a fellmonger who had been a friend of her husband.

Mrs. Elizabeth Fayrey, the widow of a prominent stapler, was known to the Johnson brothers as an efficient businesswoman who knew exactly how to ask the right questions and also how to keep herself from being cheated out of even a penny. She often sent gifts to Sabine, the wife of John Johnson. By the regulations of the Staplers Company she was allowed to ship thirty sarplers of wool a year, presumably from England—a sarpler being a large sack of coarse canvas, each sack holding eighty tod of eighty pounds each. At the same time John Johnson, an active senior partner in a firm, was permitted to ship thirty-five sarplers. So Mrs. Fayrey must have carried on a considerable business.

Mrs. Margaret Baynham, who had lost two husbands and a number of other relatives, some of them from the plague, combined business efficiency with charm of personality. Whenever John Johnson crossed over to Calais he lodged at her boardinghouse, and he kept some of his records there in her countinghouse. When she came to England both he and Sir Anthony Cave were eager to have her as a guest. "The delicacy and sweetness of her letters," says the author of *Tudor Family Portrait*, "give us no hint of the very capable business woman she really was, farming hundreds of acres of land in Calais, running a comfortable boarding house for her stapler friends, and trading in wool and wine and herring with the Johnsons and other merchants of her acquaintance." Like Mrs. Fayrey, she had the right to ship thirty sarplers of wool each year from England.

A few women, at least in the early part of the seventeenth century, continued to manage large and difficult projects. In *Working Life of Women in the Seventeenth Century*, Alice Clark cited these and others: Dorothy Selkane, who applied for a patent in 1610 to dig coal on an English manor; Ann Wallwyn, who wrote the Earl of Salisbury in 1611 asking for the wardship of the son of James Tomkins because his father was dying; Elizabeth Bennett and Thomas Berry, who contracted in 1626 to supply one hundred suits of apparel for the soldiers at Plymouth; and Margaret Greeneway, a widow, who asked for the right about 1630 to complete her husband's contract for supplying the East India Company with biscuits and also the right to bring to London five hundred quarters of wheat. Her petition was granted.

Even in the latter part of the seventeenth century a woman with business ability might build a modest fortune, unhampered by laws or other outer circumstances. One woman who succeeded in doing so was Joan Dant. Left a widow, she became a house-to-house pedlar in the area of London. From this humble business she acquired the capital to open a wholesale trade with the Continent. At her death, her executor's accounts included bills from Brussels and Paris, and she was worth more than £9,000.

But the number of these successful, large-scale businesswomen seems to have been limited. About 1662 Samuel Pepys was both pleased and surprised to hear an Englishwoman, a Mrs. Bland, talking like a merchant about her husband's business. He concluded that she was as good a merchant as her husband. About this time also it is said that Englishmen were marveling at the energy and shrewdness of Dutch women. Details like these suggest that middle-class women in England did not choose to conduct businesses as they had once done. And with the Restoration in 1660, the ladies of the English court, as well as others who wished to be considered fashionable, were cultivating idleness and frivolity.

Women in Business, Gild Members: Small Affairs

$\overline{\text{W}}$ H I L E women were flourishing in large-scale business, an amazing number of them were engaged in business on a small scale in many parts of England. And again, some view of earlier centuries seems a necessary approach to the Tudor Age. Girls of middle-class families in medieval London, Sylvia Thrupp discovered, were usually encouraged to learn a trade; thus they were prepared to make their own living or to help support the family. If true in London, probably it was true in other parts of England. And about 1443 Reginald Peacock, in *The Rule of Christian Religion*, stated that a woman might be expected to help support the family as far as her other duties would permit—her other duties being to feed the children, to prepare both food and drink for her husband and his men while they worked for the family, to watch over her husband's belongings, and to cheer and comfort him when he came home from work. A connection may exist between these statements and the great number of women who were engaged in some small business in many parts of England—in Norwich, in the West Riding of Yorkshire, in York, in Oxford, and in Berkshire.

In Norwich the number of women fined for breaking some rule of trade suggests that a much greater number must have been in business. Those who paid fines in the mayor's court are listed, with their occupations, in *Leet Jurisdiction of the City of Norwich*. Early in the fourteenth century eight women were fined at one time for trying to buy and sell without first being admitted to the freedom of the city. Alice the wigmaker, Agnes the bookbinder, and Katherine

Skinner, a common huckster, were fined for the same reason. Emma the cobbler, Mistress Coyne (keeper of a victualling house), eight women who sold oats at retail, thirteen women who sold cheese, Sarah the hatter, and Oliva the goldsmith were all listed for some infraction of the rules governing trade.

In 1379 the polltax returns for the West Riding of Yorkshire listed these women by their occupations: 6 chapmen, 11 innkeepers, 1 farrier, 1 shoemaker, 2 nurses, 39 brewsters, 2 farmers, 1 smith, 1 merchant, 114 domestic servants and farm laborers, 66 websters (30 of them using that surname), 2 dyers, 2 fullers, and 22 seamstresses. In every case, Alice Clark adds (using details furnished her by Eileen Power), these were widows or women working as feme sole. In a later list of smiths in Chester (from a Harleian manuscript, "The Smiths Book of Accounts," for 1574), she cites the names of thirty-five men and five widows.

In York women were admitted to the freedom of the city and could not legally carry on trade without this admission. In the *York Memorandum Book,* edited by Maud Sellers, many were listed as shopkeepers, clothsellers, parchmentmakers, plasterers, fishmongers, stringers (makers of strings for bows), cooks, and tanners. In the whole area of Yorkshire weaving was a business so important that every household owned a spinning wheel, with the wife and daughters spinning as a part of daily life; and nearly every household wove all the cloth needed to make garments for the family. In addition, weaving sheds existed to make cloth for sale; women in unusual numbers worked in the industry both as employees and as masters; and women masters employed both men and women. According to the details given by Herbert Heaton from accounts of the alnager (an official sworn to inspect and measure cloths) for 1395–1397, the workers in the weaving sheds of Emma Earle were turning out 48 cloths in 54 weeks, from a total of 173½ in all Wakefield.

In Oxford for 1389 the poll-tax returns, reported by Alice Clark, listed an almost incredible number of women in small businesses: 37 spinsters, 11 tailors, 9 tapsters or innkeepers, 3 shoemakers, 3 hucksters, 3 washerwomen, and others who were butchers, brewers, chandlers, ironmongers, netmakers, and woolcombers.

In the time of Edward I, according to Ephraim Lipson, at least fifty women traders were established in Wallingford, Berkshire. One list named a hundred market men and twelve *feminae forenses,* or market women. Many of them lived in villages nearby and paid a yearly fee for the right to trade as members of the local gild. About the middle of the thirteenth century, according to records in the

Victoria History of the County, the burghmote rolls and the gild records indicated that many women were carrying on small businesses throughout Berkshire.

When we turn to accounts of the gilds, we find that most trade and craft gilds admitted women to membership and that large numbers of women were active in the organizations. It has sometimes been stated, but incorrectly, that women were not usually admitted to gilds; that if members, they were not allowed to wear the livery; and that they could not be burgesses or freewomen. In her introduction to *English Gilds,* Lucy Toulmin Smith said, "Scarcely five out of the five hundred [gilds] were not formed equally of men and of women. Even when the affairs were managed by a company of priests, women were admitted as lay members; and they had many of the same duties and claims upon the gild as the men." Apparently she did not mean that the membership had as many women as men, but that they were equal in privileges. She added that men and women joined in organizing gilds and that both wives and single women became members. As for the livery, in many gilds all members, men and women, wore it; and in some gilds only a selected few of the men wore it to represent the whole group in public processions and pageants. From details given earlier in the chapter, it seems clear that women in many municipalities were freewomen.

The author of *English Gilds,* Toulmin Smith, stated that eighteen gilds founded within the fourteenth century (including the Gild Merchants of Coventry and the Tailors Gild of Norwich) required the assent of women members to ordinances and their vote in the election of officers. Twenty-five gilds founded in the same general period included women as members but made no statement about their part in the management. The Palmers Gild of Ludlow, with a record of meetings as far back as 1284, was among those admitting women. At Stratford, the Gild of the Holy Cross not only admitted women to membership but provided explicitly that both men and women were to make ordinances and choose wardens. About 1307 the Gild of St. Katherine at Norwich provided that ordinances were to be made by men and women both. In 1310 the gild at Killingholme, Lincolnshire, stipulated that a woman might be provost of the group. Toulmin Smith added that in York women were admitted to the freedom, a fact mentioned earlier, and that some women were masters, hiring both men and women. At Norwich, the Gild of St. George, founded in the reign of Richard II, prescribed livery for all members, men and women. The author of *Town Life in the Fifteenth Century*, Mrs. J. R. Green, says that at Totnes, in Devonshire, women might become members of the Merchant Gild by inheritance, gift, or purchase.

In the material examined so far, no instance appears of a woman member who was denied, because she was a woman, any right we might expect her to have. A woman member had a part in the social life of the gild, whether she was single, a widow, or a wife. As a member of a trade gild, she had the right to buy and sell within the corporation; as a member of a craft gild, the right to help set standards of workmanship; and in either, probably, the right to help fix prices and wages and to limit the number of workers. Rights for a woman member were sometimes named in specific form, as if to prevent their denial—the right to become an apprentice, the right to work or trade later as a single woman, to employ either boys or girls as apprentices, and usually the right to employ journeymen. If a woman married a man of another craft or trade, she lost her membership for the time of the marriage; if she married a man who practiced her own craft or engaged in her own trade but was not a member of her own gild, the marriage usually conferred membership on him. Though a married woman who conducted her own business as if she were a woman sole might take an apprentice to learn her trade or craft, at least in Bristol, the indentures must be signed by husband and wife, as Robert Ricart informed us in his *Kalendar* about 1478. Perhaps a sound practical reason for this requirement existed: if the apprentice was to be a member of the family he was thus under full family discipline, like the children and the servants. In most gilds, it is said, a woman could carry on her husband's business after his death, and if not already a member, was admitted to full membership.

Women were admitted also to membership in some of the great livery companies of London. The Brewers Company, in the ninth year of Henry V, spent more than ninety-nine pounds for clothing, presumably liveries, for "the brethren and sisters of the fraternity. . . ." The price for admission to membership varied about 1348: men paid twelve pence, the sisters eight pence each, and a man and his wife twenty pence. A list, apparently in the fifth year of Henry V, included the names of women who had the right to wear the livery and who were credited with the payment of their quarter-age money. These thirty-nine women were maids, wives, or widows. Details on the list indicate that a husband at this time paid two shillings for himself and his wife and that single people paid twelve pence each.

The Grocers Company also had women members. At one time, perhaps about 1348, a woman who was not a member of the company but married a member was looked upon "as of the fraternity forever and [was to] be assisted and made one of us." If she became a widow, she could come to the annual dinner, paying forty pence if able to do so. But if the widow married a man outside the fraternity, she was expelled and remained outside while the marriage lasted. Records of 1348 mentioned women members for the first time.

Women members of the Drapers Company carried on the drapery business and took apprentices as the men did. Though there were probably women members earlier, an order of 1503 states that "Every brother or sister of the fellowship taking an apprentice shall present him to the wardens and shall pay 13s., 4d." An ordinance of 1505 repeated the right of the sisters to take apprentices, naming the amount of the fee; and an item of 1540 called upon the whole company to reform ordinances and "to knit together brother and sister in perfect love and charity." The sisters had the use of the best pall when they were buried, with the same ceremonies used for men members of the fraternity. The hall of the company had a ladies chamber, "a splendid room solely appropriated to the use of the sisters of the fraternity. . . ." Sometimes the women had separate dinners in their own chamber, instead of mingling with the company in the hall. This separate room for the ladies, William Herbert reported, was still maintained in the hall of the company about 1836–1837, when he was writing his history.

An ordinance of the Fishmongers Company in 1426 provided that every year on the festival of St. Peter, "all the brethren and sustren" of the group were to come in their new liveries to the church of St. Peter, there to hear a solemn Mass and to make offerings according to their devotion. The articles of incorporation as revised in the thirty-eighth year of Edward III permitted the itinerant fish-women, called "billesteres," and also "persons or women" (or their servants) who caught fish in the Thames or other running streams to sell their wares on the streets of London, if they did not keep stalls or make "a stay" in the streets.

The Merchant Tailors received their first charter from Edward III, and the charter was confirmed by Richard II about 1392. In the latter year the master and wardens were authorized to give a yearly livery "of a garment of one suit" to the brothers and the sisters,

and to carry on other business, including the making of new ordinances. The organization took the name Merchant Tailors in 1503
by letters patent from Henry VII.

The Barber-Surgeons of London, according to their historian,
Sidney Young, admitted women from the earliest times. Women entered, usually by apprenticeship but sometimes by inheritance, from
a father who was a member. Women members bound their apprentices, either boys or girls, at the hall of the company, just as the men
did. Women did not wear the livery of the company on formal occasions, but in other ways they had the same privileges, "so far as the
same were compatible with their sex." In 1890, Young added, the
group still had one woman member.

The records of the Stationers Company offer evidence that
many women after the death of their husbands carried on a printing
business in London, in the sixteenth and seventeenth centuries. (But
there is no basis for the conclusion sometimes drawn from these
records that *only a widow* could carry on a business in London and
only a business left to her by the death of her husband.) Women
apparently operated under the same rules and regulations that guided
the men. In a list of London printers about 1553 to 1640, though the
dates are approximate, Edward Arber named seventy or seventy-
two men who died and left their widows with their print shops. More
than fifty widows disposed of the shops—some almost immediately,
some in a year or two, and a number in less than four years. Four
widows kept shop about four years each: Joan, widow of Thomas
Butter, from 1590 to 1594; Anne, widow of Thomas Chard, 1619 to
1623; Katherine, widow of Henry Rocket, 1612 to 1616; and I. Orwin,
widow of Thomas Orwin, 1593 to 1597. To spare figures, the widow
of Thomas Adams continued to manage her husband's print shop
about five years; the widows of George Purslow (perhaps) and
Leonard Greene for seven years each; the widows of Walter Burre
and George Vincent, eight years each; the widow of John Standish,
nine years; and the widows of William Broome and John Helme, ten
years each. The widow of Edward Venge seems to have continued his
print shop eleven years; Elizabeth, widow of Edward Alldee, for
twelve years; Elizabeth Oliffe, widow of Richard, fourteen years; and
Alice, widow of Thomas Gosson, sixteen years. Two women did even
better: Anne, widow of Edward Griffin, continued her husband's
business nineteen years, and the widow of John Alldee for twenty-one
years.

In an age when both men and women were eager to acquire property by marriage, even the ugliest and most vile-tempered woman in London could have found an ambitious man ready to take her—and her print shop. Probably the women who went on managing the business for some years had experience from working with their husbands, and also interest and aptitude.

The women who continued to manage print shops apparently had the usual privileges and observed the usual rules—as we learn from *Records of the Court of the Stationers Company* by W. W. Greg and E. Boswell and the second volume by William A. Jackson. Several women were granted sums for their relief, perhaps as they were taking over the shops themselves. In 1622, the year the Widow Burre began work for herself, she was "content" to assign all her right in Sir Walter Raleigh's *History of the World* to Matthew Lownes and George Latham. In 1632 the Widow Griffin was fined thirteen shillings and four pence for binding her apprentice at a scrivener's shop, instead of Stationers Hall. In October, 1634, a Widow Alldee and also Bernard Alsop, printers, were warned to appear in court on a complaint that they had printed *The Soul's Preparation for Christ,* though it was already entered to Robert Daulman. Since their action was contrary to ordinances of the Stationers Company and a decree of the Star Chamber, it was decided by general consent that "their several spindles and barrs shall be forthwith taken away and brought to the Stationers Hall, as in these cases is accustomed."

Most of these women who managed print shops could read and write, keep accounts, draw up or judge indentures they made with apprentices and journeymen, and were familiar with the local laws that applied to their work. Even in medieval London, according to Sylvia L. Thrupp, women could get the basic skills in elementary schools, though they were not usually admitted to grammar schools. They needed some education for training apprentices; masters, whether men or women, had to teach them to read, write, and keep accounts (unless they already knew these things), to provide bed and board and perhaps a small sum of money, and to be responsible for their workmanship and behavior.

Women in England had no trade or craft gilds for women only, through the Tudor Age, though the woolpackers at Southampton and the silkwomen in London have been mentioned as if they were exceptions to this statement. In medieval France, according to an article by E. Dixon, five gilds were entirely in the hands of women, a large number of others had women members, the terms of employment for men and women were usually the same, and any restrictions were made to maintain quality, not to limit women. Though it has been suggested that the decline of Englishwomen in business came about because they had no separate gilds, the facts do not seem to warrant such an idea. Certainly larger causes (to be mentioned later in the chapter) were operating.

As for the woolpackers at Southampton, they were not the independent organization that seems to emerge from some accounts of them. In the introduction to the *Black Book of Southampton*, the editor uses the group as an example of the control some cities exercised over industrial affairs. Though these women packed all the wool for shipment from the port, they were chosen by officials of the corporation, and they worked under rules made for them by these officials. By the rules, twelve women were appointed to serve the merchants; they filled their "pokes or balons" with wool, and a fair division of the work was arranged. Plans were made for the women to notify each other when their services were needed. Though they were permitted to choose two from their number to be wardens, vacancies in the group were filled through nominations by the mayor and the other officers of Southampton. This system, as the editor remarked, was a strange contrast to that of the regular gilds. Whether the women could have developed their own organization in the beginning, if they had desired, seems uncertain.

The silkwomen of London, from early times into the seventeenth century, had an organization of women only, but it was not an organized gild; only the provisions for apprenticeship were like those of the gilds. Some of the women took men apprentices. They had no other ordinances, and they did not even require from their members definite standards of workmanship. Perhaps they considered themselves artists whose work could not be measured in exact ways. They converted raw silk into thread or yarn, wove this yarn into such small articles as corselets, ribbons, laces, fringes, and tassels, and sold the articles in their own shops. They did not weave large pieces of silk for garments. In earlier years the silkwomen were prosperous. Jane Langton, the widow of a saddler, was formally bound to pay merchants of Genoa more than £500 in place of her daughter-in-law, Agnes, who had died while at Stourbridge Fair. Twenty-three different women in four years under Henry VI were listed as purchasers, buying from foreign merchants directly or through brokers. During one year, Leonard Conterin, presumably a

SOVVENT ME SOVVI

1443. Margaret Beaufort, Countess of Richmond and Derby. National Portrait Gallery, no. 551. Though the identity of the sitter has long been questioned, restoration has now convinced experts that she is Margaret Beaufort. Artist unknown. By permission of the National Portrait Gallery. London, England.

[Arranged by birth dates of the subjects]

1485. Catherine of Aragon, National Portrait Gallery, no. 163. A portrait at Hardwick Hall resembles this but was made later. A miniature of the young Catherine in Vienna has been reproduced as hers, but it is extremely doubtful. Probably this is the only authentic large-scale portrait of her. Artist unknown. By permission of the National Portrait Gallery, London, England.

KATHARINE PARRE

1512. Catherine Parr. National Portrait Gallery, no. 4618. This portrait was acquired by the Gallery so recently that it is not in Roy Strong's *Catalogue* of 1969. It is now considered the only authentic likeness of this queen. Attributed to William Scrots. By permission of the National Portrait Gallery, London. England.

COUNTESS OF SHROESBURY

1518 (?). Bess of Hardwick, Countess of Shrewsbury. The National Portrait Gallery and Hardwick Hall own portraits much alike, but the one at the latter place, the earlier, is used here. Artist unknown. With the compliments of the National Trust of Great Britain.

1520. A woman bearing the name, "Duchess of Suffolk," is the subject of a Holbein drawing at Windsor Castle. But this mature woman seems to date from the 1530s, when Catherine, Duchess of Suffolk (born in 1520), was still a child. No authentic picture of Catherine is available; the miniatures reproduced as hers are doubtful; so is a picture that was at Christie's in 1938. This woman, in earlier Tudor dress, represents those whose likenesses are unobtainable or whose names are unknown. Reproduced by gracious permission of Her Majesty Queen Elizabeth II.

1537. Lady Jane Grey. National Portrait Gallery, no. 4451.
Artist, Master John. By permission of the National
Portrait Gallery, London, England.

Right Honorable and most Vertuous
Lady MARY SIDNEY, wife to the late
deceased Henry Herbert Earle
of Pembroke &c.

Simon Passeus sculpsit L.   Are to be sold by Io Sudbury
and Geo: Humble in Popeshead
Alley

1561. Mary Sidney Herbert, Countess of Pembroke. A portrait of a much younger woman, often reproduced as hers, is really that of Lady Scudamore. Only one authentic likeness of her is known. It is the engraving reproduced here; it was made in 1618 when she was about fifty-seven. Artist, Simon van de Passe. By permission of the National Portrait Gallery, London, England.

MOLL CUT=PURSE.

See here the Prefideffe o'th pilfring Trade
Mercuryes fecond Venus's onely May'd
Doublet and breeches in a Un'form dreffe
The female Humurrift a Kickfhaw meffe
Here no attraction that your fancy greets
But if her FEATURES pleafe not read her FEATS

Pub.d by W. Richardson, Castle Street, Leicester Fields.

1584 (?). Mary Frith, or Moll Cutpurse. Frontispiece in the Folger Shakespeare Library copy of *Amends for Ladies*, by Nathaniel Field, 1639 edition. The picture is not in all copies of the edition. Sources of the picture and the artist are unknown. By permission of the Folger Shakespeare Library, Washington, D.C.

foreign merchant, sold to eight silkwomen, the consignments being valued at thirty to about fifty-seven pounds each. In 1503 Elizabeth Langton sold to members of the royal family silk articles valued at more than a hundred pounds. Many silkwomen were wives of prominent men in London, including aldermen; the husband of Elizabeth Stockton, a silkwoman, was knighted and became lord mayor of London. Apprentices came from many localities, as Marian K. Dale stated—from Warwick, York, Bristol, and from towns in Lincolnshire. An apprentice returning home probably worked as a feme sole or a feme covert, according to the local custom.

In the fourteenth and fifteenth centuries officials in London and Parliament gave protection to the silkwomen. As early as 1368, they had petitioned the mayor of London about the competition of the Lombards. In 1455 they appealed to Henry VI in Parliament, with interesting details in the petition:

Showeth your great wisdoms and also prayen and beseechen the silkwomen and throwsters [spinners] of the craft and silkwork within the city of London, which be and have been crafts of women within the same city of time that no mind runneth unto the contrary. . . . And whereupon the same crafts before this time many a worshipful woman within the same city have lived full honorably, and therewith many good households kept, and many gentlewomen and other in great number, like as there be now more than a thousand, have been drawn under them in learning the same crafts . . . whereby afterward they have grown to great worship, and never of anything of silk brought into this land concerning the same craft and occupation in any wise wrought, but in raw silk unwrought. . . .

Now manufactured goods were being brought in, the petition continued, and it had become impossible to obtain a good quality of raw silk. The situation had caused and would continue to cause "great idleness among young gentlewomen and our apprentices of the same craft within the said city, and also laying down of many good and notable households of them that have occupied the same crafts, which be convenient, worshipful, and according for gentlewomen and our women of worship, as well within the same city as all other places within the realm."

The petition led to the legislation that silkwomen desired—a law forbidding the importation of any merchandise that competed with the work of the silkwomen, only girdles from Genoa being excepted. Twice during the reign of Edward IV and again in the first year of the reign of Richard III, similar acts protected the silkwomen. In the reign of Edward IV, a certain Dom Robert Essex petitioned the king for the right to use his frames prepared for the making of silk—frames now standing idle within the monastery of Westminster. No evidence appears to indicate that his petition was granted.

But during the latter part of the sixteenth and the first part of the seventeenth century, the silkwomen gradually became less important. In *The Description of England,* about 1577, William Harrison is said to have made a comment on the change: until the tenth or twelfth year of the reign of Elizabeth, few silkshops had appeared in London and those few were kept by women and maidservants, not by men, as "they are now." The exact source of his comment is elusive, but what he asserted seems highly probable in relation to events that preceded and followed.

A petition from the merchants, silkmen, and others trading in silk came to Charles I, November 25, 1630. The silk trade had grown great, the petitioners asserted, customs had increased, and many thousands were now finding employment through the industry. The trade had originated, they explained, with women who were formerly called silkwomen. These women had trained menservants who became members of other London gilds but were powerless to reform abuses in the silk trade. The petitioners requested two things: a charter of incorporation and also a pardon for any who might have used some past deceit in the dyeing, working, or selling of silk. Ephraim Lipson added other details—the petitioners wished "to obtain control over alien weavers who had invented looms with twelve to twenty-four shuttles worked by one man's hand" and who refused to employ English apprentices or journeymen. The petition was referred to the attorney general with the request that he prepare both the pardon for past misdeeds and articles of incorporation for the silkmen. Thus came the finale of the silkwomen. Perhaps the women lacked vision and initiative, and their organization had been washed way by an upsurging capitalism.

The demise of the silkwomen was only one of many events that record the passing of women from small business in the sixteenth century. Also there had been mutterings and local actions much earlier. In 1344, the Girdlers Company of London, according to Ephraim Lipson, ruled that no woman except the wife or daughter of a member might be employed in the business. But about 1363, Parliament, in passing a statute limiting artificers and handicraft people, exempted women:

But the intent of the king and his Council is that women, that is to say, brewers, bakers, carders, and spinners, and workers as well of wool as of linen cloth and of silk, broadsters [embroiderers], and breakers of wool, and others that do use and work all handiworks, may freely work and use as they have done before, without any impeachment or being restrained by this article.

Other restrictions were passed. In the city of York, in 1400, a new rule was adopted that only women well taught and approved by masters of the craft should be allowed to weave, lest the poor work of some be reflected on the group. At Bristol in 1461 a complaint (cited by Alice Clark from *The Little Red Book of Bristol*) was made that weavers were allowing their wives, daughters, and maidservants to weave with their own looms or to be hired by others; as a result, "many and diverse of the king's liege people, likely men to do the king service in his wars and in defence of this land, and sufficiently learned in the same craft, goeth vagrant and unoccupied, and may not have their labor to their living." So the weavers were forbidden to employ any woman not already getting a living by the craft. In 1490 at Kingston-upon-Hull the weavers ordered that no woman should do any work connected with the occupation, fixing a fine of forty shillings for a violation. In 1511 the Norwich Worsted Weavers forbade women to do any work connected with the group because they lacked the strength to do good work. Sometime in the sixteenth century the weavers gild in the city of York ordered that no man was "to teach his wife, daughter, or any other woman to weave in the said craft under pain of twenty shillings."

The causes for the decline of women workers in crafts and trades, so far as they are known, were complex and far-reaching. One cause, perhaps, was the invention of machinery or the development of methods that reduced the number of people needed, such as the looms with many shuttles managed by one worker in the making of silk.

Another cause, perhaps a major one, for the decline of women in business was the change of England from a country that exported raw material to a country that exported manufactured goods. That is, England stopped exporting great quantities of raw wool and began exporting wool cloth. This change was taking place about 1500 or a little earlier. At the same time the demand for cloth was increasing greatly, both within England and overseas.

Such shifts as these brought about the development of large-scale capitalism. In the early stage (as Alice Clark and others have suggested) industry had been *domestic:* that is, the family worked as a unit within the home, making whatever the group needed for its own use but not for sale outside the home. Next a *family unit* worked together inside the home (family including servants, apprentices, and even journeymen); the members still worked as a unit, not as individual wage earners, but they sold products outside the home. After this stage the *capitalistic system* developed: a man with sufficient money established a production center where he employed many people, bringing them from their homes and paying a fixed sum to each individual worker. Of course the three systems existed side by side. This third system removed many fathers from their positions as directors of a family workshop, it separated maker and seller, and it divided capital and labor. In England the cloth-weaving industry was the place where the capitalistic system developed first and most completely. But in any industry, such as the making of ale and beer, the development of capitalism would make it harder for a single woman or a married one working as a feme sole to get a business established.

Against a background of changes like these, the great weaving industries of the fifteenth and sixteenth centuries were developing. A weaver known as Thomas of Reading may have been only a legend. Many were real: Thomas Dolman of Newbury; Kent, Style, and Chapman of Bath; Cuthbert of Kendal; Hodgkins of Halifax; Martin Brian of Manchester—clothiers who kept many spinners, weavers, fullers, dyers, and shearmen, "to the great admiration of all who came into their houses." Others were John Tame of Cirencester, in Gloucestershire, who acquired several landed estates; his son, whom Henry VIII visited and knighted and who became lord of the manor of Fairford and three times sheriff of Gloucestershire; Thomas Spring, third clothmaker by that name at Lavenham, who willed money for completing the church and for a thousand Masses, and whose daughter was married to Aubrey Vere, son of the Earl of Oxford.

John Winchcombe, better known as Jack of Newbury, was reality enlarged by romance and legend. His part in the battle of Flodden may have a basis of fact colored by romance. Jack led to the battle either 100, 150, or 250 men—accounts differ—wearing white coats, red caps, and yellow feathers; they won praise from Catherine of Aragon, regent of England, who organized the defense against the Scots. A sixteenth-century ballad cast a glamor over the weavers' work sheds: two hundred men were weaving there, a hundred women were carding, two hundred maidens (wearing red petticoats and head scarfs white as silk) were spinning, one hundred fifty children were sorting wool—all reported in round numbers for the convenience of the balladmaker. And the women and girls were all singing as they worked! Some details about Jack of Newbury are sober fact. His three-story house, remodeled by others, is still standing, or was in the last century. He rebuilt the church of St. Nicholas at Newbury, Berkshire, left forty pounds to the church in his will, and placed there a brass memorial to his wife Alice and himself. The career of Jack of Newbury ended with his death in 1520.

After the Dissolution, some clothmakers secured and used former abbeys as weaving centers. Tuckar of Burford promised to spend one hundred marks a week in wages if he were allowed to rent the lands and the fulling mills of the Abbey of Abingdon. William Stump, who had taken over Malmesbury Abbey, filled the place with looms. In 1546, when he rented Osney Abbey, he agreed to hire 2,000 workers for clothmaking. With all this growth of the weaving industry before the middle of the sixteenth century, women might have had great difficulty establishing any business of their own.

Another cause contributing to the decrease of the number of women in crafts and in trade was the decline of the gilds. They were developing into great trading companies, like those of London, or decaying because they were less useful in the changing economic conditions, and they were being restricted by statutes. Parliament began making laws to keep the gilds from doing the things they had been organized to do. About 1546 a statute declared that certain fraternities, brotherhoods, and gilds that had been dissolved with the colleges and chantries were to become the property of the crown. Another statute, in 1547 or 1548, gave commissioners power to survey all "lay corporations, gilds, fraternities, and fellowships of mysteries or crafts incorporate," and to assign to the king all except those that might be called trading gilds. In 1548 an act relating to victuallers and handicraft men asserted that the handlers of food (butchers, bakers, brewers, poulterers, cooks, and others) had conspired to ask unreasonable prices, and that artificers, handicraft men, and laborers were organized to control the times and prices of work and to refuse to finish any work that other men had begun. In the whole statute there is no suggestion that any of the workers were women. To prevent such actions that statute established penalties—fines, the pillory, or for the third offense, even the loss of an ear. Organizations conspiring to accomplish such controls were to be dissolved, and justices of the peace were ordered to punish offenders. Another part of the statute provided that laborers should not be hindered from working in corporate towns, even if they did not live in the towns and were not freemen of those towns.

Another act about 1563 compelled the services of many kinds of workers, naming weavers, shearers, dyers, tailors, bakers, brewers, hatmakers, butchers, cooks, millers, and numerous others. It seems worth noting that this act also said nothing to indicate that women workers existed—unless the word *person* meant men and women and the word *children* meant boys and girls. Unemployed workers, if they were unmarried, were between 12 and 60 years old, and did not have property worth forty shillings a year, could not refuse to serve.

Perhaps another cause for the decline of women in industry was the change in the philosophy of men about the ownership of property and their responsibilities. Medieval men tended to assume that property was given a man in trust, to be used for the common good. As the capitalistic or the factory system developed and men had chances to make more money, owners were likely to act on the belief that their property was their own, to be used for their personal satisfaction. Probably this change in philosophy (stated by Ephraim Lipson and others) was closely connected with an urge to make more and more money. Within the sixteenth century, as Christopher Hill suggests, the earlier Catholic morality was on the defensive, and capitalistic ideas were on the offensive. As this reversal of values developed, Calvin permitted some interest; but in England, said Lawrence Stone, except for a brief period about 1545 to 1552, "interest on fully secured loans was totally forbidden until 1571." In that year Parliament recognized the need and permitted 10 percent interest. Workers were plentiful in the latter part of the century; the capitalist, the small businessman, and the farmer who was giving employment to two or three workers kept wages down and felt no responsibility for his employees. A general giving of alms seemed undesirable;

instead, churchwardens, often guided by the new philosophies, searched for "the industrious and impotent poor," resenting the control of any bishops who might hold to the older philosophy. In the last two decades of the century, capitalism won, Mr. Hill says. But one who surveys the philanthropy of the same time wonders if the victory was as complete as his article alone suggests. Many women were generous givers, and many men as well, though the men may often have belonged to the gentry and the nobility. Perhaps both philosophies continued to function on different social and economic levels.

The growth in population during the sixteenth century was probably another reason for the smaller number of women in business and industry. The figures cited by J. C. Russell in *Late Ancient and Medieval Population* indicate that there had been a great decline in population in fourteenth-century England, presumably from the Black Death and from other sporadic outbreaks of the plague. In 1348 the population had been estimated at 3,757,500 people; after 1374 it had fallen to 2,250,000; by the end of the century it was about 2,000,000. About 1430 an upturn came, but the evidence for it does not appear in the lower classes but mainly in the prosperous middle class, the gentry, and the nobility. At the end of the fifteenth century, according to figures given by G. S. L. Tucker, the population of England and Wales had risen to nearly 3,000,000; by the mid-century to nearly 3,500,000, and by 1603 to about 4,100,000. The population of London and of some other cities had increased greatly, part of the increase being caused by "strangers" or "foreigns." At Norwich, E. E. Rich estimates, "there were 1,132 'strangers' by 1567, and 4,000 by 1575. . . ." Colonies of them existed in other cities. In 1573 the number in London was estimated at 4,287 (3,160 of them being Dutch), and over 2,000 of the entire number had come for economic reasons. Though no study seems to be available on the relationship between population and the presence of women in business and industry, it seems that women appeared in numbers when population had shrunk and disappeared when more men were available for jobs.

Another cause (perhaps a minor one) for the smaller number of women (especially in large-scale trade) was the growing wealth of men in the merchant class. As they prospered, they tended gradually to become landed gentry, and by the sixteenth century they had been prospering for several generations. Gentlemen with good family connections but little money had often been seeking the daughters of wealthy merchants as wives. Many a wealthy merchant had bought for himself a manor house and had thus begun to make a gradual change in the class to which he belonged. "If, as many of the wealthier men are known to have done, he [the merchant] then assumed the role of a gentleman in his county, serving on public commissions, acquiring private hunting rights, modernizing his manor house, making arrangements to marry his daughters into gentle families, and preparing at least one of his sons for the careers that were associated with gentility, the degree of change was certainly significant," said Sylvia L. Thrupp. She added that assimilation into the gentry was probably furthered in the second generation.

Such a wealthy merchant with his manor house or manor houses might soon have an income from his lands of forty pounds or more. If a man with that income were offered knighthood, he could not refuse the honor without paying a penalty. The wife of such a wealthy merchant would have a new outlet for her energies. Instead of engaging in large-scale trading on the Continent, she could use her abilities as the mistress of one or more manors.

CHAPTER SIX

Women as Manor Wives or in Other Large Households

N O women, it seems, worked harder or needed more varied abilities— not even in the twentieth century—than the wives of the men who owned great manor houses or other great country estates. The statement is true for both the pre-Tudor and the Tudor periods, though perhaps in the earlier centuries when times were less settled, a woman assumed even harder responsibilities. When her husband was at home, the manor wife ate with him, sat by his side after the meal, discussed the management of the entire estate with him, and was both companion and business partner. In his absence she entertained his guests and, with the help of a bailiff or steward, directed the farming operations—the planting and harvesting of crops, the sale of produce, the care of animals, and the general welfare of the tenants.

As mistress of the manor, she supervised the brewing, baking, and cooking; planned the butchering; ordered foods and other necessities not produced on the premises; carded, spun, and wove woolen cloth; prepared flax and made linen cloth; embroidered; directed the making of most garments worn by members of the household; and acted as doctor and surgeon for the family and for tenants who needed her services. Sometimes she trained girls from other families in the duties of managing an estate, along with her own daughters, and at the same time gave all her children their basic education. If her husband owned several manors, as many landed gentry did, she moved the family from manor to manor so that sanitation might be improved or food supplies might be used on the manors where they were produced.

In the Tudor Age, the manor lords were often away from home, sometimes for personal reasons but usually for public duties. All the landed gentry, as well as the higher nobility, had a large share in the government of England, and for that purpose they had to spend time at the center of government or to travel about England. Some were away at war or on diplomatic missions. The greater ones, or those who were trying to grow great, were court officials, members of the Council, and judges of the king's bench or of the court of common pleas. Others were commissioners of the assize, members of groups to collect the subsidy, or they served on commissions of the peace. Some of them had to spend time at the court in London or to follow the king as he moved from palace to palace or from palace to hunting lodge, since the court followed the ruler in the sixteenth century. Three or four times a year, the justices of the assize traveled one of the six circuits into which England was divided.

Since commissions of the peace included most members of the landed gentry, the lesser nobility, and even the peers, with each list headed by a high official, it may be interesting to follow them in their duties as one example of the demands made upon men by the government. The members (who might also include some esquires) were named on a commission for one or more of the shires in which they owned property. Members of the commission were responsible for the courts of record known as quarter sessions, held four times a year, either in the county town or in another large town in the shire, and lasting a day or three or four days, according to the amount of business. A principal justice (a *custos rotulorum*) notified the sheriff about the date and the place he had chosen, the sheriff issued writs to those who should attend, and the justices and other officials brought the inquisitions, recognizances, and records of examinations they had held. Bills of indictment were drawn up and placed before a grand jury; members of this jury marked each bill either *Billa vera* or *Ignoramus;* the true bills went to a jury for trial. While the jury was working, other members of the commission handled affairs of civil administration, such as the repair of jails and other buildings, of bridges, and of highways. The indicted persons were tried, and the *custos* pronounced sentence against those who had been declared guilty. If a member of the commission attended all four quarter sessions (though no evidence appears to prove that he was required to do so) and if all were long sessions, perhaps he might spend three or four weeks at quarter sessions in a year for one shire. And he might be on a commission for more than one shire.

Members of a commission for the peace had other duties. Each might work as a single justice for certain specified kinds of cases, as one of two justices for others, or as one of several justices for other cases. At any time when the justice was in his county, a local officer might bring an offender before him. A single justice also had powers about settling disputes, deciding administrative details, or acting on matters of trade. When Conyers Read edited *William Lambarde and Local Government,* he included "Ephemeris," a record of Lambarde's work as a justice from 1580 to 1588. The list gives an excellent idea of the interruptions a justice of the peace might have, taking time from his own estate, and leaving decisions to the bailiff, the steward, or ultimately to his wife.

The system of commissions of the peace, of jail delivery, of the assize, and other commissions, produced good government at the smallest possible expense. But the system lasted because men of property had a keen interest in maintaining law and order in areas where they had landed estates. Through the centuries the pay remained almost stationary, even in a period of inflation, but the duties multiplied. Lambarde, in *Eirenarcha,* 1581, gave us evidence that Holdsworth, in *A History of English Law,* accepted and praised. Lambarde said of the duties: "how many justices thinke you now may suffice (without breaking their backs) to beare so many, not loads but stacks of statutes that have since that time been laid upon them." Of the pay, Lambarde said the whole amount was sometimes spent in "defraying their common diet." One may wonder whether the government of England could have functioned unless there had been a change in the system and enormous added expense, without the competent wives of the great landowners.

Manor wives who had to take the responsibility when their husbands were away (or if their husbands died suddenly) might have found help in four early treatises on management. All were written in the thirteenth century, all attempted to bring together the practical wisdom of the time, and all four proved useful to men and women well into the sixteenth century. One of them, Walter of Henley's *Husbandry* (said by doubtful tradition to have been translated into English by Bishop Grosseteste for the use of Margaret, widow of John Lacy, Earl of Lincoln) emphasized such ideas as knowing the value of every part of the property, selecting servants carefully, changing seed, improving the land, testing the yield of milk cows, and buying and selling at the proper seasons. Two other anonymous treatises might also have been useful: *Husbandry,* with advice on keeping accounts, checking the accounts of the bailiff, and keeping the estate self-sufficient; and *Seneschaucie,* with explanations of the duties of the steward, the bailiff, and other workers on the estate.

Grosseteste's *Rules,* or *The Rules of St. Robert,* were perhaps actually written for the Countess of Lincoln. The work seems well adapted to inform a man or a woman who had to take over the management of a great estate. The writer advised such a person to know his lands; to estimate the harvest of grain and the expenses; to budget the profit for bread and ale, kitchen expenses, wines, wardrobes, wages of servants, and so on. He must command his marshall to keep an eye on all members of the household, and to dismiss the incompetent, to keep peace in the hall, to distribute alms wisely, and to receive and care for all guests. He must command his knights and other gentlemen who wore his livery to wear it at all meals.

Rules for keeping order appear next, too many to repeat here. "You yourself should always sit at the middle of the high table, that all may plainly see that you, as lord or lady, are there. . . . Have your marshall keep order especially in the hall. . . . Watch until all have been served and then attend to your own food. . . . Unless hindered by sickness or fatigue, eat in the hall before your people." Every year at Michaelmas, the good bishop advised, plan the time when you will go to each manor and the number of weeks you will spend there, to use the food available and to avoid the burden of debt. More rules follow about the management of affairs outside the manor or castle.

Writers of the sixteenth century who advised the mistress of a simpler country home on her duties help to clarify our ideas about such a household. One of these writers was Thomas Tusser, who published *Five Hundred Points of Good Husbandry* in 1557 and added to a later edition *The Points of Housewifery.* Elementary as his work may seem to the modern reader, it was reprinted many times in the sixteenth century and a half dozen or more times in the early part of the seventeenth century. The good housewife, he said, rises at dawn and sees that her maidservants do the same. She gives all her servants a breakfast of pottage with a little meat "when the daystar appears." She is friendly with them but she demands efficient work. She manages well the brewing, baking, washing, and the dairy work. At dinner she gives her servants plain but nourishing food. She organizes well the work to be done in the afternoon and the evening. She has at hand a good supply of herbs and other simple remedies for illness. She nurses her own children and disciplines them with a birch when it is necessary, beating them till they cry for mercy and promise to behave. She educates them, considering their individual aptitudes as she does so; and if they have the inclination, she teaches them music.

William Harrison's account of brewing, in *The Description of England*, about 1577, gives us authentic information because he tells us how his wife and her servants made their beer once a month. They ground on their own quern eight bushels of malt and added to it a half bushel of wheat meal and a half bushel of oatmeal. They heated an eighty-gallon vat of water and ran it through the mixture of meals. They used two more vats of water in the same way, adding at some time a pound and a half or two pounds of hops, a half ounce of orris, and an ounce of bayberries finely powdered. Using these quantities, they made three hogsheads of good beer at a cost of about twenty shillings; at least it was good enough for people of his income—about forty pounds a year. The amount lasted his household for a month. But he did not mention the size of his household!

Though Tudor women were energetic and resourceful, earlier fifteenth-century women had established a tradition of coping with even greater problems. An outstanding earlier woman was Isabel, who became the third wife of James Berkeley about 1424. He had the right to Berkeley Castle by the will of his uncle, Thomas, Lord Berkeley, who had no son to inherit the property but did have a daughter Elizabeth who was his direct heir. Elizabeth had married Richard Beauchamp, the Earl of Warwick; and after the death of Berkeley, she and her husband seized the castle. In the struggle that followed James Berkeley was threatened with great violence, so that he and his sons had to stay at home to defend their rights. So the Lady Isabel traveled to London and became "the sole solicitor of her husband's law causes." In her letters she exhorted her husband not to give in to his opponents: "Sir, your matter speedeth and doeth right well. . . . At the reverence of God, send money, or else I must lay my horse to pledge and come home on my feet: keep well all about you till I come home, and treat not without me." James Berkeley lacked ready money, like many others in the period, but he borrowed from Nicholas Poyntz, pledging for the debt the furnishings of his private chapel.

Then Isabel went to Gloucester, "following her husband's business as a solicitor"; there she was seized by an enemy of her husband and imprisoned in a strong castle "against all right and conscience." Because Margaret, the Countess of Shrewsbury (the one immediately responsible for her imprisonment) was in favor with Henry VI, the order for Isabel's release was slow in coming. About the time it was issued by the king, she died in captivity. According to her biographer, John Smyth, she was murdered; Isabel's son William brought suit, accusing the Countess of Shrewsbury.

Paston women, also in the pre-Tudor period, are better known than Isabel Berkeley, because they speak directly to us in *The Paston Letters,* edited by James Gairdner; but they too did not always behave like sheltered women. Margaret, wife of John Paston (1421–1466), was an intrepid defender of the family property because her husband had to spend much time away from home. He was a member of Parliament; probably he lived for a time in the household of Edward IV; he spent much time in London or elsewhere on legal business for Sir John Fastolf; later he was the chief executor for Fastolf; and he had to be away for legal business of his own. Lord Molyneux had laid claim to the manor of Gresham, though William Paston had bought it and then willed it to his son and heir, John. The Duke of Norfolk was making trouble about Fastolf's will because he had not only made John Paston his chief executor but also the heir to his Norfolk and Suffolk property; and the Duke of Suffolk was claiming the manor of Drayton. These men were formidable opponents.

Margaret Paston, the wife of John Paston, was at Gresham with only twelve other people when a thousand men of Lord Molyneux came to recover it. They were armed with cuirasses, guns, and bows and arrows; they brought mining instruments, long poles with hooks used for pulling down houses, ladders, pickaxes, and pans of fire. They broke down the outer gates. Soon they began undermining the room where Margaret had stayed, refusing to come out. Finally they carried her out of the building by force. They took all the movable property, cut down the door posts, and left ruin behind them. When her husband petitioned the king about the attack, he estimated the loss in movable property alone at two hundred pounds.

Margaret Paston also carried on for weeks a running battle against the men of the Duke of Suffolk, with each side trying to assert ownership by collecting rent from the tenants at Drayton and by holding the usual manor court. But only her chaplain and a man named Thomas Bond were willing to support her about the manor court. Sixty or more of the duke's men reached the place first. When Paston's men admitted that they came to hold court, the duke's men arrested Bond and tied his arms as if he were a common thief.

Because the justices of the peace were coming the next morning, presumably to hold quarter sessions, Margaret was on hand early to talk with them before they went to the shire hall. In the presence of these leading men of the country, property owners who came to look into conditions but most of them neither judges nor lawyers, she explained the situation. When she had finished her story, the justices gave the duke's bailiff a "great rebuke" and sent the sheriff to estimate the forces gathered on each side. After considering carefully, they overruled all demands against the Pastons, ordered Bond to be set free, and severely censured the Duke's men. Margaret's husband, who was usually appreciative and who had been concerned about her health, must have given her high praise for this victory.

In contrast to Isabel Berkeley and Margaret Paston, the lives of Tudor women seem comparatively normal. The times were usually more peaceful, but a lack of ready money, struggles about the ownership of property, and some other conflicts continued. Sir Robert Plumpton (1453–1523) was one of those who did not lead serene lives. Other heirs were trying to claim his property, partly through scandalous stories about his illegitimacy, because his father and mother had had a private marriage ceremony. He was called from home at least twice to help put down outbreaks in Yorkshire, and often he had to be in York or in London because of lawsuits about his property. At times his enemies even managed to have him in prison.

On November 27, 1502, his wife Agnes, the daughter of Sir William Gascoigne, was writing him about troublesome tenants their son had ousted. The archbishop had ordered the son to "set the tenants in again" or he would send the sheriff to reinstate them. In December she was writing again: "God knows that I have made as great labor as was possible for me to make, to content your mind in all causes; and now I have made the usance [an agreement to pay interest] of £ xx and sent you. . . ." She added that the archbishop had asked an indictment against their son William and sixteen of his servants, an official had presented the bill of particulars, but the "quest" [the jury who acted on the bill] refused to indict them. The archbishop was trying to get the names of those who refused to indict, so he might punish them. So far, she had not been able to get a copy of the indictment.

In March of 1504 she wrote her husband that she had arranged for the money he needed and was sending it by John Walker. She hoped he would not be displeased because she had not sent it sooner, but she had done the best she could. As Sir Robert's troubles came partly from other heirs who were making claims to his property, Agnes wrote again in April, 1504, expressing surprise that she had not heard from him and that he was not working to protect himself. "They" think they are going to take the Whitsunday farm. She begged him to remember his great charges and hers and to take action to end the trouble; for Edmund Ward had been arrested and "they" had "stopped the country" so that no man would deal with any of the Plumpton servants, not even to buy wood. Again she urged him to get some word to the sheriff, so that the "prossess" might be stopped. She was sending him a copy of the letter from the under-sheriff, a copy of the causes, and a letter from a certain Ellyson. Unless he took some action, she did not know how his house could be kept, for she didn't know how to levy one pennyworth.

What he did, we do not know, but a little later the persistent and concerned Agnes wrote that she and the children were in good health and that they had been able to sell oaks, ash trees, and also holly. This letter seems to be her last. After giving her husband a large family, as well as defending his property, she died before the end of 1504.

As his second wife, Sir Robert Plumpton married Isabel, the daughter of Ralph, Lord Neville, in September, 1505. Isabel also had her troubles; she bore them with less patience, perhaps, but with similar concern. At one time she wrote to her husband: "Sir, I have sent to Wright of Idell for the money that he promised you, and he saith he hath it not to lend . . . and so I can get none nowhere. And as for wood, there is none that will buy, for they know ye want money, and without they may have it half for naught, they will buy none. . . ." Later in the letter she said they refused to buy unless they could get "tymmer" [timber?] trees, and if she sold them, his wood might be destroyed. She added: "And your Lenten stuff is to buy, and I wot not what to do . . . for I am ever left of this fashion. . . . Sir, for God's sake, take an end, for we are brought to beggar-staff, for ye have not to defend them withal."

Perhaps Isabel Berkeley, some two generations earlier, or Margaret Paston would have known what to do. But conditions for the Plumptons eventually improved. Though Sir Robert was in prison and without money, and Isabel may have been imprisoned with him part of the time, Henry VIII freed him when he came to the throne and restored his property.

Women on the smaller English manors were often excessively busy, even when they were not combating enemies or trying in other ways to fend off disaster. When Sabine Saunders, niece of Sir Anthony Cave, married John Johnson, she soon became involved. About 1544, some three years after their marriage, John and Sabine acquired Glapthorne Manor in Northamptonshire. He was a member of the firm of Johnson and Company, with his younger brother Otwell as an active member, and Sir Anthony Cave as an investor in the business. John had been an apprentice to Sir Anthony, and probably Sabine had been trained in her uncle's household at Tickford Priory, Buckinghamshire.

Since manor households were almost self-supporting, Sabine Johnson supervised the cleaning, polishing, planning of meals, cooking, spinning, weaving, sewing (most garments being made at home), brewing, and baking. She looked after the flower garden; the vegetable garden (and probably the herb garden); the dairy with the making of butter and cheese; the feeding of pigs, poultry, cattle, and horses; the collecting of eggs; and the sale of excess produce at some market town—perhaps Oundle, about a mile and a half away. Of course she had servants, but she carried the responsibility. Her husband's business required much travel—travel in England buying up wool and skins, and travel between London, Calais, Bruges, and Antwerp. Whenever he was away, she managed his big farm, "directing the woolbinding and winding and sheep-shearing, buying cattle and horses, collecting the tithes and rents, seeing to the repairs of the barns and houses, paying the bills and keeping the accounts, and looking after village affairs generally." John required of her the same careful accounts that he kept in his own business, according to Barbara Winchester in *Tudor Family Portrait*, and thus she had to itemize every penny or even farthing that she spent. Fortunately for Sabine, by 1550 at least, she had a young bookkeeper, Thomas Eggilsfield. And if she spent her earlier years at Tickford Priory, she had been well trained.

During the busy years at Glapthorne, Sabine was also bearing her children. The ones mentioned came in 1542, 1544, 1546, and 1548, though the records do not indicate whether these were boys or girls; and in 1550 came the birth of "a boy who lived." Since permanent records did not always include children born dead or those who died shortly after birth, the total is uncertain. But she escaped the fate of the many young wives who died in childbirth.

But Sabine Johnson was not so vigorous in the defense of their common interest as some earlier women had been. About 1545 when there was trouble over tithes and an appeal in Chancery was decided against John, Sabine called for her husband's help. If he did not come home by the day she expected the parson and another man to call with their demands, she served notice on her husband that she planned to be away herself, "because I will not be troubled with them, for two enemies against one woman is too much." Margaret Paston would not have said so.

In the middle and the latter part of the sixteenth century the household of Sir William Petre (a secretary to Henry VIII, to the Protector under Edward VI, to Mary, and an officer and counselor to Queen Elizabeth) must have been a demanding one for his wife. The activities mentioned here were managed by his second wife, Anne Browne, daughter of Sir William Browne, a lord mayor of London. In 1539 Sir William had bought Barking Abbey from the king at the market price and added to it other Essex properties nearby. Then he demolished the Abbey and built a great country house, Ingatestone Hall. He also kept a substantial house in Aldersgate, London.

Sir William was an effective worker in securing the surrender of at least thirty-three religious houses, was one of a number to draft the bill for the Six Articles, and in 1543 became a secretary of state —a position he held under three rulers until 1566. In 1544 he was an aid to Catherine Parr when she was regent of England; in 1545 he went as an ambassador to the Emperor and became a member of his king's Council; in 1547 he became keeper of the great seal. These activities must have demanded some time overseas and much time at court.

Lady Anne Petre's problem, as the wife of an official closely connected with the court, was that of entertaining guests or supervising the household when her husband was away from home. F. G. Emmison in his biography of Sir William Petre has given us vivid details. In November, 1548, the Princess Mary stopped overnight, a visit that meant fifty guests. When Mary returned home a few days later, she stopped again. This time Sir William had gone to court, and Lady Petre had to manage alone. Again, in 1550, while the master was overseas, the Princess Mary sent word that she would be coming over from New Hall, Boreham, a chief residence of hers, near Ingatestone Hall. Of course a princess traveled with a retinue, and again there were many guests.

In July, 1552, while the host, Sir William, was away and his wife was entertaining Lady Norwich (the godmother of her daughter), William Cecil arrived, bringing his wife with him; other special guests were Mr. Tyrell of Warley, and Mr. Worthington, with "six mess in the hall of their servants," each mess being served food for four. Also haymakers, carpenters, and laborers had to be fed. The total for the occasion was eighty people.

From 1548 to 1552, the Petres had twenty outdoor and indoor servants, mostly concerned with providing food and drink. The food consumed seems ample, if not excessive. In 1552 the hall ovens turned out 20,000 loaves of bread. In the same year (with figures for one week missing and with no meat served in Lent) the family, servants, and guests consumed 17 oxen, 14 steers, 1 bull, 4 cows, 29 calves, 129 sheep, 1 teg [a yearling sheep], 54 lambs, 3 boars, 9 "porks," 5 hogs "killed for bacon," 3 goats, 7 kids, 1 stag, 13 bucks, and 5 does—the total for 46 weeks.

On July 19, 1561, when Queen Elizabeth was making a royal progress, "Sir William and Lady Petre with the servants in their grey marble liveries" awaited her arrival that day about noon. She and many members of her court stayed till July 22. Before her arrival, Lady Petre had supervised the preparation of the royal suite, buying thirteen ells of green taffeta sarcenet to line the curtains, having the best hangings brought from the Aldersgate House, and buying a quarter pound of "fusses" for "perfuming of chambers." Of course this work was only a small part of the total preparation; she needed extra food supplies, including spices and special delicacies, more servants, and lodging ready for members of the court. Sir William Petre estimated his expense at more than £136, a modest amount compared with other entertainments for the queen.

Lady Mildmay, born Grace Sherrington about 1552, and married to Anthony, son of Sir Walter Mildmay about 1567, was another who became the mistress of a great house and who entertained royalty. She left a record of herself in a journal that has never been published in full. Her account of her education suggests what may have happened to many other later Tudor women. During her girlhood at Laycock Abbey, Wiltshire, she was trained by a poor relative and a member of the household—a Mrs. Hamblyn, whom Grace's mother (a sister of Sir Francis Walsingham) had trained. Mrs. Hamblyn was strict, religious, witty, and wise; she could express herself well in talk or in letters. Grace delighted in her company. She never allowed Grace to be idle but would have her cast accounts, write an imaginary letter to some person, do needlework, or read Turner's *Herbal* and Vigon's work on surgery. She also used every means to guide Grace against wanton talk or behavior. Grace's own mother, like many other Tudor parents, was also a strict disciplinarian. She used to beat her daughter severely, especially to cure her of lying, and the daughter recorded the fact without any sign of rancor or question.

Grace's marriage (arranged for her with Anthony, son of Sir Walter Mildmay, of Apethorpe, Northamptonshire, before she was fifteen) was mentioned in an earlier chapter as an example of the father's power to decide about his son's marriage. Anthony hesitated because he wished first to see the world. If the son refused, the father said, he would never help him about another marriage. So they became man and wife. But Anthony used most of their living allowance in seeing the court and the world while Grace lived quietly with her husband's parents. Her husband was away much of the time for about twenty years.

She refused to go with the great ladies who wished to take her to festivals at court, for fear she might be tempted to evil. She made and practiced a daily schedule of activities: systematic reading of the Bible; practice on the lute, "setting songs of five parts thereunto"; singing psalms and prayers; confessing her sins, which (she said) were always ready to turn her from God and goodness; and doing artistic work by making her own designs of fruit or flowers instead of copying them.

After Sir Walter Mildmay died in 1589, Anthony arranged his financial affairs, paid off his debts, and settled his wife as the mistress of Apethorpe. In 1596 he was knighted. Grace gave much of her time to helping the sick and the needy, basing her activities on the principle that no able-bodied person on the estate was to be relieved except by his own work. Because sick people in the country had no provision for medical help, she used her own knowledge of medicine and surgery. She established loans and small bonuses to help families in distress; she apprenticed poor children so that they might learn trades; she willed money to help people learn how to weave; and she gave aid to poor scholars. Thus she worked with vigor, benevolence, and sound sense.

In 1603 King James honored Sir Anthony and Lady Grace by a visit to Apethorpe. The dinner served him was expensive, appealed to the taste, and was "beautiful to the eye, the lady of the house being one of the most excellent confectioners." In August, 1612, while he was on a hunting trip, the king paid another visit to Apethorpe.

Lady Mildmay planned all the details of her household with unusual care. At any time when she was to be absent she left explicit directions about the work to be done while she was away. Her careful records indicate also that most provisions were supplied from the estate, all bread being baked and all beer or ale brewed at home. Her table of work for each of her ten household servants was unusually exact. Of the three maids, one was to serve as cook; one to tend poultry, make butter and cheese, and look after some other necessities; the third was to be a chambermaid or to do other work at the pleasure of the mistress. Of the seven men, one was to bake and brew; one to tend the grounds; one to arrange for the supply of beef and mutton and to act as a "cater" or a general purveyor of foods; two were to attend on the mistress of the house; one was to serve in the buttery (and in his absence one of the maids or the brewer might take his place); and the seventh was to serve as a footboy.

Like most sixteenth-century English families of status and property—even the most devout and moral ones—Sir Anthony and Lady Grace Mildmay believed in a bountiful supply of good food and drink, and their portraits present them as richly and tastefully dressed. She had a well-organized household; she was practical and sensible in aiding the poor, as well as giving them medical and surgical assistance. She had been educated in the growing Puritan tradition, with great emphasis upon the direct study of the Bible and with the belief that to spare the rod is to spoil the child. Her background was nonhumanistic, with no emphasis on Greek, Latin, or the classics, even in translation.

At the end of the century, mistresses of manor houses lived much as earlier ones had done, although the times were more settled. Margaret Dakins Hoby, whose *Diary* covers the time from August, 1599, to August, 1605, left detailed evidence. Born in 1571, she was trained in the "godly" and Puritan household of the Earl of Huntingdon. At her first marriage (to Walter Devereux, younger brother of the Earl of Essex), the Earls of Huntingdon and of Essex and her father, Arthur Dakins, had contributed funds to give the young couple Hackness, in Yorkshire. Margaret's first husband was killed in battle in 1591. In 1592 she married Thomas Sidney, brother of Sir Philip, leaving the undersized, cantankerous Posthumous Hoby as a rejected suitor. Her second husband and also the Earl of Huntingdon died in the same year, 1595. With the help of letters from Lord Burghley, Hoby renewed his suit. In May, 1596, a cousin reminded

Margaret that she would need powerful friends because a brother of the Earl of Huntingdon was bringing suit in Chancery to recover Hackness. She and Hoby were married at his mother's house in Blackfriars in August, 1596.

Though material considerations had apparently been the basis of the marriage, Margaret was a busy and a loyal wife, with firm religious habits. She began the day with prayer and Bible reading, retired to her own room twice a day for prayer and meditation, attended public prayer and a lecture by the chaplain of the manor, and took part in the singing of Psalms (a usual service in a Puritan household). She closed the day with private prayer. Twice on "the Lord's Day" she went to church, where she was in charge of a class of women. Her chaplain often read aloud to her and the maids while they were working, and in his absence another member of the household would do the reading.

As a part of her own reading, she mentioned sermons, the writings of eminent divines, the *Book of Martyrs*, the work of William Perkins, Thomas Cartwright, and Thomas Bilson, and a herbal (probably one by Gerard, published in 1597), a lecture on rhetoric, and two political tracts on Essex. She also read "a little of humanitie" (whatever the vague phrase meant), but she made no reference to any specific classics.

With this program of religious duties and reading, it might seem that Margaret Dakins Hoby would have time for little else. But that idea would be quite wrong, judging from her own reports. Among the household tasks that she and her maids performed, she mentioned pulling hemp, weighing wool, dyeing stuff, winding yarn, spinning both wool and hemp, making wax lights and oil, taking her bees and seeing her honey put in order, making aqua vita with a still, preserving damsons and quinces, and preparing sweetmeats and gingerbread. They made most of the clothing for the family and also tapestries and other hangings for the house. Margaret herself gave simple medicines and performed simple surgeries, not only for her entire household including the servants, but also for the workmen and their families. Once she dressed the wounds of two patients twice a day for two months, she made a salve for a beast with a sore, and in general she was both nurse and midwife without expecting any reward for her services.

Like other manor wives, she supervised outside activities when her husband was away. He must have been away much of the time; he was a member of Parliament, a member of the Council of the North, a member of a commission for the subsidy, and a justice of the peace, who might have to deal with small offenses at any time and also attend quarter sessions. He was also a self-appointed scourge of recusants (those who failed to attend regular church services), and he brought many law suits. When he was at home, she spent much time discussing business affairs with him. In his absence she looked at the wheat, and watched the workmen, including those who plowed and sowed rye. She supervised the planting of corn, estimated the amount in hand for provisions, and also saw that some rooms were "made handsome" for storing corn. She was often in the hayfields; she bought sheep, had trees planted, and talked with the new miller about his duties. She kept the accounts, paid the wages of servants and other workmen, signed leases, received rents and fines, and drew up business statements. In short, when her husband was away, she did all the work of a modern farm manager.

She had some amusements, though when she found any time for them is a mystery. She mentioned bowling, fishing, singing and playing on the "alphorion," going to fairs, and driving out in her coach to "take the air" or to see friends. She had many visitors, and usually six or seven guests on Sunday. She made visits to York and to London occasionally; once she mentioned dining in London with her mother-in-law, Lady Elizabeth Russell.

Lady Margaret Hoby did not have the problems of earlier women who tried to defend the property of their husbands against forcible seizure, and she did not mention any worry about finances. She did suffer once the riotous behavior of some guests, self-invited ones, who had a grudge against her husband. In August, 1600, William Eure and his companions came to supper, carried on loud and lascivious talk larded with oaths during household prayers, remained all night, became drunk, and before they left, broke windows and insulted their host. Though Sir Posthumous was at home, he found himself unable to cope with them; but he took a complaint to Star Chamber and they were fined £100 for their uncivil behavior. Margaret Hoby did not have to handle this problem, as she might have done in the less quiet days of Margaret Paston.

Other women in the sixteenth century managed large households or great estates and were outstanding administrators—Mildred Cooke Cecil (Lady Burghley); perhaps her sister, Anne Bacon; Catherine, Duchess of Suffolk; and Bess of Hardwick (Countess of Shrewsbury). Among royalty they included Margaret Beaufort, Catherine of Aragon, Catherine Parr, and Queen Elizabeth, who managed the realm, it might be said, as if it were her own great household. But they were not manor wives, who superintended farming operations while the men were away conducting affairs of the government: they were official hostesses or they were administering great properties of their own. Margaret Parker, efficient and gracious hostess for Archbishop Matthew Parker, helped her husband entertain on a royal scale at Lambeth Palace and the Old Palace in Canterbury.

Social attitudes and human nature both change slowly. After the last Tudor had gone to her final rest, occasional women were intrepid, resourceful, able in administration, and keenly interested in both politics and literature. One of them, Brilliana, born about 1600, was the daughter of Viscount Conway and became the third wife of Sir Robert Harley. After her marriage she lived at Brampton Bryan Castle in Herefordshire. Her abilities were well summarized in *English Folk* by Wallace Notestein; she revealed herself in *Letters of the Lady Brilliana Harley*, published by the Camden Society. An illness that she complained of soon after her marriage never left her, but she managed to bear three sons and four daughters. At times she was bedfast for days, being so weak that she had to dictate her letters to others, scarcely finding the strength to sign them. She followed the actions of Parliament with keen interest. She had wide literary interests, recording her views in letters to her son Ned at the university, exchanging opinions with him on sermons and religious pamphlets, telling him that Francis Godwin's *Man in the Moon* reminded her of Don Quixote, and expressing her delight in French books: "for I had rather read anything in that tongue than in English."

Since Brilliana and her husband sympathized with the Roundheads, the Royalists laid siege to Brampton Bryan Castle while her husband was attending Parliament in London. Rising above her physical weakness, she managed to secure arms and ammunition, food supplies, and additional men for the defense of her "house," as she called her castle. From July 25, 1643, to the end of August, she maintained "a remarkable defense," interwoven with parleys and a petition to the king. Finally the besiegers retreated to Gloucester. But when forces gathered against her castle again in October, her delicate health broke completely under the strain; she died before the end of the month.

Perhaps the Lady Brilliana Harley was the equal of many of the great Tudor women. But in the sixteenth century great women were numerous, and women with vigor and initiative were pressing forward on many levels of society and in many areas of achievement.

Women, from Royalty to Common Folk, in Various Activities

T H E vigorous Tudor women who appear in this chapter were breaking the conventions of passive behavior on all levels of society except the lowest (where records are lacking) and in every kind of activity. A few were artists connected with the court; some were fearless martyrs; others, supporters of religious reform; a number were lawbreakers; many were philanthropists.

Of the women artists or alleged women artists connected with the court, no one did distinguished work, at least while in England. One who was often listed earlier as Alice Carmylyon was apparently a man, Ellys or Alexe Carmylyon. The payments for him, in *Letters and Papers of . . . Henry VIII*, were low—as if for a woman—but they merely indicate his status as a craftsman. When he disappeared from the payrolls in 1546, his pension was assigned to Sebastian Henyon, a man. The jobs mentioned for him (such as gilding vanes for the Tower, and working on an arbor) were men's work, and though he was called a milliner, in that age milliners were usually men. A recent authority, Edward Croft-Murray, assumes without question that Carmylyon was a man. An early statement by John Gough Nichols that "the woman, Alice Carmylyon, seems to have been a miniature painter," was only an unguided thrust into darkness.

A curious item in *Letters and Papers* for 1540 names a woman painter, Katherine Maynor, describing her as a widow and a native of Antwerp, who was given letters of denization on November 11, 1540. But no other information about her appears, either in available government records or in books on Renaissance artists. While a forgery is possible, surely a forger could do better than to name a woman artist! Perhaps she was only a scribal error—but the details are strangely definite.

Susanna Hornebolt (1503–1545) is a less shadowy figure who had some early ability as an artist. She was the daughter of Gerard and Margaret Hornebolt of Ghent, and her father was one of the best illuminators of his time. In 1528 her father brought his family to England. Though it is recorded that Susanna married John Parker, a yeoman of the robes in the royal household, and that she was the wife of a sculptor named Worsley when she died at Worcester, she seems never to have been on the list of the king's payments. But on the Continent she had been praised. Dürer recorded the fact that she was with her father at Antwerp in 1521 and wrote of her: "Master Gerard, the illuminator, has a daughter about eighteen years old named Susanna. She has illuminated a Salvator on a little sheet, for which I gave her one florin. It is very wonderful that a woman can do so much." According to Wilenski, Dürer also said that he drew her portrait. Both Guiccardini and Vasari praised her work as an illuminator, and Guiccardini called her a miniature painter, adding that she had been invited to England by Henry VIII and that she lived there wealthy and honored. But no evidence appears either for wealth or for honor. It seems uncertain whether her early talent failed or whether she was not appreciated in England.

Lavina Terling (Flemish form, Teerlinck) fared better at the English court. She was born at Ghent or Bruges and was the daughter of Simon Bennick, painter and miniaturist. About 1545 she came to London with her husband, G. Teerlinck. The first item about her in *Letters and Papers,* in November, 1546, reads: "Mrs. Levyna Terling, paintrix, to have a fee of £40 a year from the Annunciation of our Lady last past, during your majesty's pleasure. Preferred by My Lady Harbert." In 1546 the Lady Herbert (wife of Sir William Herbert, later Earl of Pembroke) was the queen's sister, Anne Parr. Payments to Lavina Terling, according to the Household Accounts in the *Trevelyan Papers,* continued through the first three years of the reign of Edward VI, listed as quarterly wages of £10.

The next official item about her was one of the letters patent issued by Queen Elizabeth, October 10, 1559: "Grant for life for her service to Henry VIII, Edward VI, Queen Mary, and the present queen, to Livina Terling of an annuity of £40, and arrears of an annuity granted with her appointment during pleasure as nurse by letters under the signet . . . ," November 28, in the thirty-eighth year of Henry VIII. Since this last date is that of the original appointment, it seems clear that *nurse* is a blunder for *paintrix.*

Lavina Terling is said to have given Queen Mary a limning of the Holy Trinity as a New Year's gift in 1556, to have presented Queen Elizabeth in 1558 with the "queen's picture finely painted upon a card," and to have received in return a gilt casting bottle, used for sprinkling perfume. But the evidence for these details seems uncertain. In 1562 the queen did receive from Mistress Terling among her New Year's gifts "the personne and other personages fynely painted," and the painter received from the queen a gilt cup with a cover. The term "fynely painted" refers to miniature work.

In the past, two beautiful miniatures—the portraits of two little girls, one holding an apple, the other a red carnation—were considered the work of Lavina Terling. But in 1952, Graham Reynolds, deputy keeper of paintings at the Victoria and Albert Museum (where the portraits now are) reported that both have been established as the work of Isaac Oliver. Two other works in the Pierpont Morgan collection were formerly ascribed to Lavina Terling, but according to the same expert, one is too late to have any connection with her, and the other is the work of Nicholas Hilliard. So we have no examples of her work—only the knowledge that she was working under four Tudor rulers; that after neglect, she was compensated by Elizabeth; and that she was an individualist who worked as an artist when few women made the effort.

One other artistic woman, Esther Inglis, is sometimes called a miniaturist and certainly was an expert calligrapher. She was born in France, perhaps at Dieppe, in 1571. Her Huguenot parents fled from that country shortly after the massacre of St. Bartholomew, in 1572. By 1578 her father was master of a French school in Edinburgh. Tradition suggests that she was a nurse to Prince Henry when he was with the Earl of Mar and the Countess Dowager and might thus have been considered a member of the royal household; but the word *nurse* has crept into records where it does not belong. Considering her status, it seems more likely that she taught the prince handwriting.

The artistic and literary work of Esther Inglis remains in manuscript books. When Dorothy J. Jackson published a preliminary sketch about her in 1937, she had traced forty-two books, one title being used twice: three concerned emblems; twenty were selections from the Bible, chiefly from the Psalms; sixteen were collections of moral verses; one was a political tract; one a religious treatise; and one a book of prayers. About twenty-eight of the known volumes have dedications—to Queen Elizabeth, in 1599; to Anthony Bacon, the Earl of Essex, Robert Cecil, William Petre, and others. James I received dedications in 1605 and 1615; Prince Henry twice in 1608 and once in 1612; Prince Charles in 1615 and twice in 1624. From the many dedications to distinguished people it seems probable that she expected and received payments for her books. Some of her dedications perhaps grew from the fact that she and her husband, Bartholomew Kello, "a minister of God's word," came to London in 1606, and a little later they were in Willingale Spain, Essex, where he served as a rector for several years. By 1615 they were back in Edinburgh, where Esther lived till her death in 1624.

The manuscript books written and illuminated by Esther Inglis have "exquisite workmanship." But her creative ability was limited, though "there is no other woman of the period whose signed manuscript books survive in such large numbers." Many other calligraphers, both men and women, including Elizabeth Lucar, Jane Weston, and Georgette de Montenay in France, were working about this time. Esther's lack of individuality may be illustrated by her use of a book of emblems that Georgette de Montenay had published in two editions, one with a Latin and one with a French title. Using the one with the French title, Esther made a rather faithful manuscript copy, "her minor changes in spelling and decorative detail being incidental to the liberties necessary in freehand copying. She included a long dedicatory letter of her own composition to Prince Charles, and a portrait of herself, with laudatory verses [others had written about her], immediately following that of Georgette de Montenay. She changed a few names among the emblem dedicatees and used a different title-page compartment . . . and altered the face of the queen building a house of books, which in the original represented Jeanne d'Albert, Queen of Navarre, to Elizabeth, Queen of Bohemia. In Esther's copy the queen wears a different bodice and shoes as well as enlarged Jacobean ruffs." Though the work was not highly original, as usual it was beautifully executed.

Four manuscript books by Esther Inglis are among the holdings of the Folger Shakespeare Library. The earliest, *Les CL Pseaumes de David*, 1599, in which the writer seems to have used all the variations of her beautiful handwriting, is dedicated to Prince Maurice of Nassau. It is a small volume bound in velvet, with a coat of arms and an embroidered border on the cover. Two of these four books have the same title: *Octonaries upon the Vanitie and Inconstancie of the World*. The earlier of the two is dated January 1, 1600, the later in 1607. The fourth volume, *Argumenta Psalmorum Davidis*, 1608, is a tiny book, bound in velvet, with the royal coat-of-arms in tiny seed pearls on the cover. It is dedicated to Prince Henry.

Esther Inglis was also respected for her scholarship by such friends as Andrew Melville, head of Glasgow College and later rector of St. Andrews University; Robert Rollock, Principal of St. Andrews; and Bishop Joseph Hall, Dean of Worcester. These men, as well as Esther's husband and others, wrote verse praising her virtues and her skill.

Of the women who have been discussed here for their interest in artistic work, not one came from English parents or was born in England. In the first part of the century most men who were painters or were doing any decorative work were also aliens. Perhaps Sir Thomas Elyot had reason for his complaint in the *Governour* that English parents discouraged their children from learning to draw and paint and that Englishmen who wished to have such work done must employ foreigners.

❖

A discussion of the intrepid Tudor women would be incomplete without the martyrs, regardless of the faith of each. At least one woman who died for her religious opinions and who was considered important enough for inclusion in the *Dictionary of National Biography* suffered martyrdom under each Tudor ruler: Joan Boughton under Henry VII, Anne Askew under Henry VIII, Joan Bocher under Edward VI, Joyce Lewis under Queen Mary, and Margaret Clitherow under Queen Elizabeth.

Margaret Clitherow and Anne Askew, women of opposing faiths, have been selected for discussion because each was unyielding and each refused to save herself by incriminating others. Margaret, known as the martyr of York, was the daughter of Thomas Middleton, sheriff of York; in 1571 she married John Clitherow, a wealthy tradesman and butcher who was also the treasurer of the city. Though her husband conformed in religion, she became an ardent Catholic about three years after her marriage. Finally she was arraigned at the York assizes, and accused of harboring Jesuit and seminary priests and of hearing Mass. She refused to plead because she could not do so without incriminating others, including her servants and her children, who would be forced to testify against her. Finally, after long efforts to convert her had failed, a judge pronounced the special sentence for such a refusal, known as "peine forte et dure":

> You must return whence you came, and there, in the lowest part of the prison, be stripped naked, laid down, your back upon the ground, and as much weight laid upon you as you are able to bear, and so to continue three days without meat or drink except a little barley bread and puddle water, and the third day to be pressed to death, your hands and feet tied to posts, and a sharp stone under your back.

Because she was pregnant, her condition being confirmed by four matrons, her execution was delayed and others tried to persuade her into pleading. She was finally executed on Lady Day, March 25, 1586. Nearly four hundred years later Pope Paul placed her name on a list of forty candidates for sainthood. Now she is Saint Margaret.

Anne Askew is probably the best known of the women martyrs in sixteenth-century England; and though she held the opposite faith, she ranks with Margaret Clitherow in her endurance. She belonged to an old Lincolnshire family and was married early without her free consent. She was literate enough to know the Bible well, to dispute about it with the clergy at Lincoln Cathedral, and by her own account, to surpass them in arguments. After she and her husband had two children, he put her out of his house because she offended the priests.

Anne appeared in London in 1545, perhaps having come in the hope of securing a formal separation from her husband. Charles Wriothesley (who recorded events in *A Chronicle of England,* with little personal reaction) said that Anne Askew, with several men, was arraigned at the Gild Hall, June 13, 1545; but when no witnesses appeared against her she was dismissed. On June 18, 1546, Anne and three men were again arraigned at the Gild Hall. They confessed without a jury trial, and all were condemned to be burned. On June 19, Anne was taken to the Tower and racked; "she was sore tormented, but she would not convert for all the pain." On July 16, Anne and others were taken to Smithfield, but as they still refused to recant, they were burned.

Otwell Johnson, a merchant, writing from London to his brother John, July 2, 1546, reported that Mistress Askew and others were arraigned at the Gild Hall and sentenced. Two men recanted and might escape, but Anne and one man remained steadfast. Johnson added: "and yet she hath been racked since her condemnation (as men say) which is a strange thing in my understanding. The Lord be merciful to us all."

Thus Wriothesley and Otwell Johnson corroborated some details given by John Foxe in *Acts and Monuments,* and Foxe did collect information from eyewitnesses as well as spend time and money checking events. In the Tower, Foxe reported, Anne was questioned about encouragement she had received from persons of influence—the Duchess of Suffolk; the Duchess of Sussex; the Duchess of Hertford; Lady Denny; and Lady Fitzwilliam. She refused to incriminate them, saying she knew only what her maid had told her. They racked her a long time, Foxe reported, but because she lay still and did not cry, Rich and Wriothesley "took pains to rack me with their hands, till I was nigh dead." In his recent biography of *Thomas Cranmer,* Jasper Ridley reported that Chancellor Wriothesley took hold of the rack himself because the lieutenant of the Tower refused to torture her. Even the details about the racking that are given as if quotes from Anne herself become credible if we realize that the maid who brought money to Anne in prison may have taken down details as Anne dictated them; later, perhaps, she gave them to Foxe. These events took place in the period after the passing of the Six Articles, when Stephen Gardiner followed the trial of heretics, including Catherine Parr.

Foxe added details about the execution, details that might have been noted by eyewitness. Anne was so weak from torture that she had to be carried in a chair to the execution and fastened to the stake with a chain around her body. But as Shaxton (one of those who had recanted) preached, she was not too weak to comment, telling him when he was right and when he was wrong. Here she seems in character—like the younger Anne who had disputed with the clergy in Lincoln Cathedral.

Anne Askew was a difficult woman—opinionated, headstrong, utterly lacking in tact or humility. But she was also a vigorous, fearless Tudor woman who did not follow the courtesy books or the opinions of religious leaders. She made her own rules—and followed them. Because Anne Askew and Margaret Clitherow refused to incriminate others, Catholics, Protestants, and also those who think that no religious view matters might honor them alike as sisters in heroism.

Persecution for religious heresy, says W. K. Jordan in *The Development of Toleration in England,* rests upon the idea that there is "an ascertainable body of religious truth which must be believed in its entirety in order to attain salvation." Those who hold this belief without any doubts, he adds, will persecute deviants to prevent infection from spreading, and will persuade themselves into believing that heresy is not compatible with a healthy social order. They will also demand that the secular ruler, who holds his office by divine commission, help the church in its support of religious truth. Thus persecution becomes a duty, carried on by men who in other relations are humane.

Other Tudor rulers had made small distinction between inner belief and outer action when they demanded conformity. Queen Elizabeth, a pragmatist, not usually given to the defense of absolute truths, kept asking what policy would be effective in a given situation. As a result, she made some advances about heresy. She did not wish to meddle with the consciences of her subjects or "to make windows into men's souls." She was concerned with the question whether men and women were loyal to the state and the crown, and she wished to punish only traitors—those who might refuse to bear arms against a foreign prince or foreign invaders. On some occasions she greeted proudly those Catholics she considered loyal to her and the government of England. But people were executed for heresy in her reign, and religious tolerance was not fully recognized in England until the end of the seventeenth century.

❖

It seems unfair to discuss women martyrs without mentioning the women who served their religion in life, not death. Of course Catholic women harbored priests and arranged Masses, but under rulers who made their work necessary, it was also secret. Both men and women worked to establish moderate reform or to put a firm foundation under Puritanism. A number of Puritan peers and knights were members of the Privy Council. After summing up their varied and successful efforts to support their beliefs in the first thirty years of the reign of Elizabeth, Lawrence Stone added that the support of the women was an "extremely important factor," because great numbers of them were actively religious. As examples he named Elizabeth, Countess of Lincoln; Frances, Countess of Sussex (who founded Sussex College to advance Puritanism); Anne, Countess of Warwick; Lady Elizabeth Russell; Lady Grace Mildmay; Lady Anne Bacon; Lady Margaret Hoby; and Catherine, Duchess of Suffolk. Of course many others he did not name were actively working to further their religious views.

An earlier zealous worker for moderate religious reform was Catherine Parr. She held formal religious discussions for her attendants at court, exerted as much influence as she dared on Henry VIII while she was queen, arranged for the translation and publication of the first volume of the *Paraphrase* by Erasmus, edited *Prayers or Meditations* (with many editions under that title and many others as the *Queen's Prayers*), and wrote *The Lamentation of a Sinner*. Anne Stanhope Seymour, wife of the Protector, also the Duchess of Somerset, sponsored the second volume of the *Paraphrase* by Erasmus after the death of Catherine Parr. She received many dedications acknowledging her services to the reform of religion; she was a vigorous worker in support of her religious views.

Catherine, Duchess of Suffolk, was a zealous worker for her religious views. During her first marriage to Charles Brandon, Duke of Suffolk, she appointed reforming chaplains for their household; she gave alms to Ridley, Latimer, and Cranmer after they were sent to prison and before she went into exile on the Continent; she furnished financial aid to Martin Bucer when he was teaching at Cambridge and also held conversations with him and attended his lectures; she was giving a home in her London house to John Foxe when he was ordained a deacon; and she invited Hugh Latimer to live as her guest at Grimsthorpe for several years about 1550. There he preached to her servants his seven well-known sermons on the Lord's Prayer, as well as twenty-one other sermons there or in parishes nearby.

Probably she gave Miles Coverdale, the distinguished translator of the Bible, a home in her household about 1559 to 1664, when he was without an income except for her aid—though the idea, so far as this writer knows, has not been suggested before. One biographer of Catherine, Evelyn Read (using the household accounts available for about two years centering around 1561) did report that a Mr. Coverdale, "a preacher," lived at Grimsthorpe and apparently tutored the children; but she merely wondered whether he was a relative of the well-known translator. Many-sided evidence, however, suggests that he was really Miles Coverdale. When he returned to England from exile about 1559, he had no public position and little or no money. These facts about his finances appear in letters he wrote to Sir William Cecil and Archbishop Parker just after he had the news of his appointment, about 1564, to St. Magnus in London. His purpose in writing the letters was to ask if he might accept the position without paying the customary first fruits, because of his age and his poverty; he had not held any ecclesiastical appointment, he explained, since he was deprived of his bishopric—a loss he had suffered when Mary came to the throne in 1553. Hence he needed financial help about 1559 to 1564. It seems unnecessary to offer evidence that Catherine would have been both able and glad to help him; one of her aims was to further the religious life of the common people by providing them with the Bible in English. The household accounts also state that Mr. Coverdale was on the payroll for £5 a quarter, and one might safely assume that he had no living expenses. At that time a young, undistinguished tutor and chaplain might have received one-fourth as much, or less. Miles Coverdale must have been physically able about 1559 to 1564 to direct the education of Susan and Peregrine (the children of Catherine by her second husband) or even to use on them the birch rod mentioned in the household accounts; for he was appointed to St. Magnus and preached in London until 1568. Since he had an unusual knowledge of theology and of languages, as we know from his translation of the Bible, he might be considered an excellent teacher for the children of Catherine, Duchess of Suffolk.

In addition to these efforts to further her religious views, Catherine did what she could to help the common people on her estate and in neighboring parishes to find their own faith. Instead of conforming under Queen Mary, she risked her worldly possessions and her life by going into exile on the Continent.

Four daughters of Sir Anthony Cooke used their unusual education or gave other services to advance their Puritan views. One of them, Lady Elizabeth Russell, has already been mentioned for efforts to support her religion. Lady Anne Bacon, another daughter in the Cooke family (the wife of Sir Nicholas and the mother of Sir Francis Bacon) sheltered Puritan preachers at Gorhambury, as Lawrence Stone suggested. She also used her education in languages to support her religious views. She translated and published sermons of Bernardino Ochino because she considered his ideas and his attitudes important. In an earlier volume she translated six of the sermons, and in a later volume all of them were her translations from the Italian. Later she translated from Latin to English Bishop Jewel's *Apology or Answer in Defense of the Church of England*. His version was intended for people on the Continent. She translated it for those people of England who did not read Latin readily—or perhaps not at all. When she sent copies of her English version to the author and to Archbishop Parker, each approved it without the change of a single word. Later Anne Bacon tried to aid the Nonconformists in another important way: Archbishop Whitgift wished to stop controversy by a vote of Parliament that would forbid reading, preaching, or catechizing in private houses. She appealed to Lord Burghley by asking him for an interview and by writing him later to explain her personal view further. But in spite of her efforts, these privileges were forbidden.

Her sister, Mildred Cecil, later Lady Burghley, spent time at court for many years because she was the wife of the great statesman under Queen Elizabeth. There she seems to have quietly exerted influence for the nonconforming Puritans whenever she could. Often she aided preachers who shared these views in securing appointments. Though she had the ear of a sympathetic husband in the many pleas she probably made for the Puritans, and though his high position in the state gave him chances to aid them, it also limited him because he had to consider the views of the queen. A fourth daughter of Sir Anthony Cooke, Catherine Killigrew, was the wife of Henry Killigrew, the able diplomat. She was active in the support of Edward Dering, who had "the intense evangelical experience by a first-generation Protestant of justification and union with Christ, through the renunciation of 'will-works' and of the world, and the exercise of a lively faith," according to Patrick Collinson, "and the consuming desire to convey this experience to others." When the Privy Council was delaying action about stopping his public lectures at St. Paul's, though the queen wished them stopped, Catherine Killigrew and her husband, Sir Henry, were among those supporting him. Finally the queen herself ordered the end of the lectures.

The letters Catherine Killigrew and a number of other women received from Edward Dering were spiritual consolation. The women were seeking assurance about the doctrine of election and leaned on evangelical preachers, Patrick Collinson suggests, "as a Catholic would lean on his confessor." Other women who received spiritual support from Dering included Lady Mary Mildmay, Lady Golding of East Peckham, Kent, Mrs. Mary Honeywood, and a Mrs. Barrett of Bray. Probably all of them were ready to support the evangelical preachers whenever they could. Among the women who sought spiritual consolation from Thomas Wilcox, a prominent preacher, were Bridget (Countess of Bedford), the Countess of Sussex, Lady Anne Bacon, Lady Walsingham, Lady Mary Grey, Lady Fielding, and Lady Rogers.

Anne Locke is an interesting example of a middle-class woman with enough education to publish translations from the French and enough vigor to further her religious views. As the daughter of Stephen Vaughan and his second wife, she had come honestly by heresy, individuality, literacy, and literary expression; and her first husband, Locke, also belonged to a literary family. John Knox wrote letters of spiritual guidance to her and to a number of other women, with a warmth of friendship that seems strange for him. Thirteen letters he wrote to Anne Locke about 1556 to 1562 are extant. When he urged her to join the saints in exile, she finally did so, although she had to bring with her two small children; but in 1559, after the accession of Elizabeth, she returned to England and her husband. After the death of her first husband, she became the wife of the fiery theological rebel, Edward Dering, about 1572 or 1573. After his death in 1576, she married Richard Prowse some time before 1583. In 1560 she had published a translation, *Sermons of John Calvin*, dedicating it to Catherine, Duchess of Suffolk. In 1590 she published a translation from Jean Taffin, *Of the Marks of the Children of God*; she dedicated it to the Countess of Warwick. Though Nicholas Udall made his comment earlier, perhaps she was the type of woman he had in mind when he wrote his preface to the first volume of the translation of the *Paraphrase* by Erasmus. At that time, he said, good people were joining to spread religious truth in various ways: "some by translating good books out of strange tongues. . . . Noble women and those of the lowest class join in this work."

❁

In a period when women were vigorous individualists, it is only rea-
sonable to suppose that some of them would be operating outside
the law—either as sinners disobeying the laws of God and the church,
as criminals breaking the laws of the state, or as flaunters of all law.
A few will be mentioned briefly before the discussion of such major
figures as Jane Shore, Penelope Rich, and Mary Frith, who have been
selected for their varied activities. Among the husband-killers, an
early one was Agnes Cotell (ca. 1518–1523), who strangled her husband
with the help of two yeomen, burned his body, and almost at once
married Sir Edward Hungerford of Heytesbury, Wiltshire. Another
was Alice, a stepsister of Sir Thomas North. Having carried on an
affair with John Mosbie, a steward in the North household, before
her marriage to Thomas Arden of Faversham, Kent, she connived
with Mosbie and two hired assassins to kill Arden. Her story is the
basis of the play, *Arden of Faversham*. Another well-known killer
was Frances Howard, who used the influence of her powerful relatives to secure a dubious annulment of her marriage to the young
Earl of Essex, to bring about the poisoning of Sir Thomas Overbury
in the Tower, and eventually to achieve her own marriage to Robert
Carr, Earl of Somerset.

Among the major sinners, Jane Shore is already familiar to
many. She was the mistress of Edward IV and then of Lord Hastings.
In 1483 when Richard III condemned Hastings to death, he accused
Jane of sorcery, sent her to the Tower, took her property, and brought
her before the bishop of London as a harlot. She did public penance.
Sir Thomas More, born in 1477 or 1478, may have witnessed that
penance, but probably he listened to the accounts of adults who had
been present. His analysis of her character was based on accounts of
those who knew her:

Nothing in her body that you would have changed, but if you would have
wished her somewhat higher. Thus say they that knew her in her youth. . . .
Now is she old, lean, withered, and dried up. . . . Yet delighted men not
so much in her beauty as in her pleasant behavior. For a proper wit had
she, and could both read well and write, merry in company, ready and quick
of answer, neither mute nor full of babble, somewhat taunting without displeasure and not without disport . . . she never abused to any man's hurt,

but to many a man's comfort and relief; where the king took displeasure she would mitigate and appease his mind; where men were out of favor, she would bring them in his grace. For many that had highly offended, she obtained pardon. Of great forfeitures she got men remission. And finally in many weighty suits she stood many men in great stead, either for none or very small rewards, and those gay, rather than rich. . . .

She appeared in many literary efforts later. In 1563 Thomas Churchyard published, in Baldwin's *Mirror for Magistrates,* "Shore's Wife," perhaps the best of his poems. In 1593 Anthony Chute issued a work about her, *Beauty Dishonored.* In 1597 Drayton included a poem about her in *England's Heroical Epistles.* On August 28, 1599, the *History of the Life and Death of Master Shore and Jane Shore, his Wife,* as it had been acted by the servants of the Earl of Derby, was entered on the Stationers Register. A ballad about her, attributed to Thomas Deloney but probably composed much later, appeared in Percy's *Reliques.* On February 2, 1714, Mrs. Oldfield took the part of Jane in *The Tragedy of Jane Shore,* by Nicholas Rowe. In the same year, an anonymous twenty-page work, *The Life and Character of Jane Shore,* dedicated to Mrs. Oldfield, came from the press in London. She was often presented as the victim of an arranged marriage to William Shore.

Another major breaker of laws was Penelope Devereux, sister of the Earl of Essex, and for years the wife of Robert, Lord Rich. Like Jane Shore, Penelope was a woman of unusual beauty. With her other brothers and her sister she was a ward in the strict Puritan household of the Earl of Huntingdon. Her guardian and Lord Burghley, Master of the Court of Wards, arranged for her a marriage to Lord Rich, in November, 1581. Since Sidney's *Astrophel and Stella* may have been largely a literary exercise, not a biographical document, perhaps one cannot accuse her of lawbreaking at this time, but one cannot be sure that she was the helpless victim of an arranged marriage.

When she became the mistress of Sir Charles Blount about 1589, bore him a daughter, gave Rich a son the next year, and then gave birth to three sons and two daughters whom Blount acknowledged in his will, she was breaking the law of the land, violating the teachings of her church, and also forsaking the canons of taste that might suggest loyalty to one man or the other. On November 14, 1605, she was given a decree of divorce from Lord Rich, but the decree stipulated that neither of the two was to marry again while the other was living. Before the next month was over, on December 26, 1605, William Laud performed a marriage ceremony for Penelope Rich and Charles Blount. As the marriage was a violation of canon law, the children of Blount were not made legitimate. But it brought one penalty that Penelope had escaped during years of open adultery: she was no longer received at court.

There is no doubt that Penelope was guilty of inciting rebellion against the government about 1598 to 1601. She wrote a "malapert" letter to the queen; it was published in 1603 with the *Apology*, written by her brother, after the queen had boxed his ears. On February 8, 1601, she was with her brother at Essex House, taunting him with having lost his valor and telling him that his friends and followers thought him a coward. So he made the fatal sally. Possibly he would not have gone out without her urging. At least she did what she could to make him a traitor.

Mary Frith (1584?–1659), highway robber, receiver of stolen goods, friend of highwaymen, but probably no prostitute, was the strangest lawbreaker of all. The daughter of a shoemaker in the Barbican, she refused the discipline of an education her parents had planned for her. She was placed in domestic service, but she hated housework and the care of children. She was fond of animals; a picture in the 1639 edition of *Amends for Ladies* shows her with a lion, a monkey, and presumably an eagle. She began dressing as a man, even wearing a sword; soon she became notorious as "a bully, pickpurse, fortune teller, receiver, and forger." When she did penance at St. Paul's Cross about 1612, for wearing men's clothing, she made a great show of remorse; but she had consumed three quarts of sack and was only maudlin. Though two highwaymen, Captain Hind and Richard Mannan, were among her special friends, probably her interest in them was not sexual but occupational. On her thieving expeditions she usually took with her a dog she had trained to help her. Eventually she employed a whole gang of thieves and became known as Moll Cutpurse.

When she robbed General Fairfax on Hounslow Heath she had the misfortune to wound him in the arm and to injure or kill two horses that his servants were riding. She was convicted and sent to Newgate, but after she paid the general £2,000, she was released. Usually more fortunate in her robberies, she became a woman of property with a house in Fleet Street. This house was her residence, a place of business for her gang of thieves, an informal tavern for them, and a pawnshop. For a price, owners could recover the rings or jewelry that her thieves had stolen from them. In her complex personality she had some elements of a philanthropist; for on Sundays she visited Newgate and Ludgate jails, taking food and money to the prisoners.

Early in her career, Mary Frith had already earned a place in the popular literature of the day. In August, 1610, *A Book Called the Mad Pranks of Merry Moll of the Bankside,* by John Day, was listed in the Stationers Register, though it seems not to have been published. In 1610 or 1611, when she was about twenty-seven years old, Middleton and Dekker presented her tolerantly in their play for the Prince's Company, *The Roaring Girl.* In 1618 Nathan Field dealt with her in *Amends for Ladies,* a work that was reissued in 1639. About three years after her death, an anonymous writer published *The Life and Death of Mistress Mary Frith.*

Mary Frith's strange life ended when she was about seventy-five years old. In spite of her long career as a breaker of law, she was buried with the rites of the Anglican church after services in St. Bride's, near her home in Fleet Street. Certainly she was a vigorous individualist. Few women at twenty-seven, or any other age, could boast of having a play written about them for the Prince's Company. When she is judged solely by her own standards and aims, perhaps her life was a success.

Organized philanthropy really originated in the sixteenth century, said W. K. Jordan, author of *Philanthropy in England, 1480–1660.* The movement began with efforts to relieve the suffering of the poor and later developed into massive endowments intended to root out the causes of poverty. Both the funds and the organization of efforts came largely from private sources. The philanthropists were deeply religious people and were motivated by religion, Jordan explained, but they did not work through the church, believing its organization to be unprepared for such efforts. Instead, they dealt with poverty through secular channels. As the wealthy city merchants and the gentry found that they could use their wealth to bring about social change, they began doing so. The influence of the London merchants spread over England, the efforts gained speed in the reign of Elizabeth, and the aristocracy also contributed to the relief of the poor. Lawrence Stone said: "Indeed, none of the great landlord *elites* of the twentieth century can compare with the Elizabethan aristocrats in the matter of social responsibility." Both men and women were philanthropists, but perhaps the women contributed even more than the men.

Before the Tudor Age, with its organized philanthropy, a few men and women made large individual contributions to the public welfare. One of the women who did so was Elizabeth, Countess of Clare, in the fourteenth century. After inheriting the family estate and the title, she transformed University Hall into Clare College, Cambridge, giving it funds and a body of statutes. Another pre-Tudor philanthropist was Agnes Forster, who worked first with her husband and then as a widow for the reform of London prisons. In 1463 she turned over to the authorities the addition she had completed for Ludgate prison; she also gave them complete plans for the reform of all the prisons in the city. These plans, according to Paul M. Kendall, were adopted.

/ In the early part of the sixteenth century, men as different as Sir Thomas More, Thomas Starkey, Thomas Becon, and Henry Brinkelow had been pleading the cause of the poor. About 1573 to 1576 William Lambarde's College of the Poor was a limited plan because he wished to provide only for "poor, honest, and goodly persons who have been three years resident in the parish" and who had been examined for piety and antipapal sentiments. Many others, so far as one can determine, wished to help all the poor and also to remove the causes of poverty. In the 1580s John Bowes wrote two tracts in which he suggested that trades be taught to girls and that grammar schools with broadened curriculums be opened to the poor. About this time also citizens were giving funds to care for the helpless in institutions, to furnish marriage portions for destitute girls with no families, and to endow apprenticeships.

Within this general background many women were making unusual contributions. An early philanthropist in the sixteenth century was Thomasine Bonaventura Percival, the poor Cornish girl who acquired wealth by her marriages to three merchants of London. In her will about 1513 she provided food and other necessities for the poor prisoners in all the jails of the London area, for the needy people in hospitals and lazarhouses, and for the future of boys and girls she brought up as alms. In Cornwall, according to Walter H. Tregellas, she gave time and money to "repairing of highways, building of bridges, endowing of maidens, relieving of prisoners, feeding and appareling the poor," and similar benefits; she built a substantial bridge at Week Ford; she built and endowed a free school at Week St. Mary.

Among the women philanthropists was Anna Fiennes, Lady Dacre (died 1595) who founded Emmanuel Hospital in Tothill, Westminister, and assigned property in York for its support. Her foundation proved to be a growing concern, with a school for poor boys and girls built much later and with a considerable annual sum paid to the city of London as the holder in trust of the charity. Many Tudor women built almshouses: they included Margaret, Countess of Cumberland; her daughter, Lady Anne Clifford; Anne, Countess of Warwick; and even Bess of Hardwick, Countess of Shrewsbury. Apparently they did not inquire into religious beliefs but only into human need.

Lady Burghley did much to help the unfortunate, keeping her plans unknown even to her husband until he discovered them at her death. She provided books, scholarships, and some other benefits for Cambridge and Oxford Universities and for the college at Westminster. She had arranged for twenty poor people in Cheshunt to have food and drink on the first Sunday of each month; was sending clothing to the poor in Cheshunt and in London at various times in the year; and had been providing money for bread, cheese, and drink for four hundred or more persons in all the prisons of London. She assigned "a good sum" to the Haberdashers Company, so they could lend twenty pounds apiece to six poor men of certain occupations in Rumford, Essex; she arranged another sum for loans to men in Cheshunt and in Waltham. She sponsored a weaving project, giving wool and flax to women in Cheshunt, asking them to make it into yarn and bring it to her, so that she might see their way of working. Sometimes she had them weave the yarn into cloth, paid them more than the product was worth, and then gave the cloth to the poor. Shortly before her death she bought a quantity of wheat and rye to be given to the poor in a time of scarcity and rising prices. In this plan she seemed to have no theories about limiting her help to the deserving poor—only the realization that people might be hungry but unable to buy food.

Alice Owen, who spent most of her life under the Tudors, established later a school at Islington, on the spot where she had narrowly escaped death as a child. In 1608 she bought eleven acres of ground, built a chapel and almshouses with the school, provided for their support, and established rules for the school. The value of her trust funds increased: in 1878 the school was expanded by royal assent into two schools on a new site in Owen Street, one for three hundred boys, the other for three hundred girls. She also contributed to Christ's Hospital and to Oxford and Cambridge Universities.

Elizabeth Carey, Lady Falkland (born in 1585, though her experiment came after the Tudors) founded industrial schools in Dublin, where she had gone when her husband became lord-deputy. She brought together weavers of linen and of woolen cloth and others who could teach trades. From beggar children she selected about a hundred sixty who were seven years old and a few who were even younger. She put them under masters to learn the trades for which they seemed best suited. Accepting older boys and girls also, she arranged for them to learn trades requiring more physical strength or greater development of the mind. Years later she learned that her husband thought her work, if it had been well managed, would have been of great benefit to Ireland. But she failed because she was not a good executive.

In *A Survey of London* John Stow named women of that city who were noted for their philanthropy. One of them was Avice Gibson, who (by license of her husband Nicholas) founded a free school at Radcliffe, near London, and provided £50 for the support of sixty children of poor men; she also founded almshouses for fourteen poor, aged persons, with a quarterly allowance for each of them. Margaret Dana, widow of William Dana, ironmonger, gave £2,000 to be lent to young men of her husband's company, with the interest on their borrowings to be used for other charitable purposes. Dame Mary Ramsey, wife of a lord mayor of London about 1577, being "seised of lands in fee simple," made a gift, with the consent of her husband, of £243 a year for the relief of poor children at Christ's Hospital. After she became a widow, she confirmed the gift and added to it.

W. K. Jordan also named some individual women who were

honored for their part in such work. Alice Avenon, about 1570, left a bread charity for the poor of London. Helen Branch, the wife of Sir John Branch, former lord mayor of London, was praised at her death, about 1594, for her contributions that centered on her own parish, St. Mary Abchurch, in London.

In the period from 1480 to 1660, 4,699 women made individual gifts or bequests, in addition to the joint gifts they made with their husbands. The greatest number of women donors were in London and in Yorkshire—1,100 and 1,121—and Kent was next with 857. The women came from all ranks of society, though few of them had the status of artisans or husbandmen. Over half were widows, a number were spinsters, and about a fourth were married women who bequeathed their own property with the consent of their husbands. Some of the women, Jordan says, were "great and farsighted donors," and had independence and maturity of judgment. In their plans for giving, they were even more secular than the entire group of benefactors; though the gifts were not made through the church, they were inspired by the idea of Christian love. Apparently, then, the change from the medieval Catholic emphasis on good works as essential to salvation, to the Protestant stress on a state of grace, did not completely hinder the development of philanthropy, and neither did the shift in philosophy about ownership as a trust used for the common good to ownership for the benefit of the owner.

PART THREE

Escape from Limitations through Education

CHAPTER EIGHT

Women with a Sound Classical Education

T H E Tudor Age, especially as the sixteenth century advanced, was well populated with women interested in education and literature. In contrast, the period between the Norman Conquest and the accession of Henry VII had been like an uninhabited desert so far as women with these interests were concerned. Only five or six women are mentioned in histories of literature for a period of some four hundred years. One of the earliest women was Marie of France, "the first woman poet to live in England," but she wrote her lays for a court that was still French, that of Henry II. In the fourteenth century, Christine of Pisa (Du Castel by her marriage) refused an invitation to come from France to England, but she exerted an influence by English translations of her works. In 1489 Caxton published her *Book of Feats of Arms and of Chivalry,* and when the classical education of women was progressing, *The City of Ladies* appeared in 1521. Perhaps Joan Beaufort, daughter of John of Gaunt, encouraged literature when she lent her nephew (the future Henry V) copies of *The Chronicles of Jerusalem* and *Godfrey of Bulloigne.* Other ladies of rank owned small libraries; for example, Anne Stafford, a mother-in-law of Margaret Beaufort, willed her several books. Jane Beaufort, a granddaughter of John of Gaunt, unconsciously inspired a captive prince from Scotland to write *The King's Quair.* Dame Juliana Berners, or a woman with a similar name, compiled, mostly from the works of others, *The Book of Hawking, Hunting, and Blasing of Arms,* with editions in 1486 and 1496.

Two mystics left records in the fifteenth century. Margery Kempe, after she had a vision of Christ in human form, recovered from insanity and finally turned to a life of contemplation. As she was unable to read or write, two men, perhaps her son and a priest, wrote down for her the story of her life. Juliana of Norwich, probably a Benedictine nun, recovered after receiving the last rites and had "a living vision of the Crucifix." She began to learn sixteen lessons of divine love. With a limited education, she had the power of self-analysis, a philosophic mind, and literary skill. Anglicans and Catholics agree that her *Revelations of Divine Love* established her as one of the greatest English mystics. Of the women named here, five are called writers, two of them by courtesy only. Of the three bona fide writers, Marie of France and Christine of Pisa wrote in French, but the latter was never in England; only Juliana of Norwich was truly English and also had some claim to greatness.

In contrast to these early women, spanning a period of four hundred years, a great number of women participated in the educational and literary life of the sixteenth century. Important causes for the change lie in the development of the Renaissance, in the ideas of the early English humanists, and especially in the theory and practice of Sir Thomas More in educating his daughters. About 1500 a distinguished group of men who had been studying mainly in Italy—William Lily, William Latimer, Thomas Linacre, William Grocyn, and John Colet—were returning to England. They had been exploring theology, medicine, and the classics; some of them were improving their knowledge of Greek or of Renaissance Latin. In 1499 Erasmus came to England for the first time and quickly formed an intimate friendship with More and Colet.

Heady with draughts of the new learning, these men began assuming, in various degrees according to their special interests, that they might reform religion by a return to scripture and the writings of the early Christian church, and that they might improve secular life by a study of the classics. But they needed the original text of both sacred and secular manuscripts, not versions corrupted by the errors of scribes, the ignorance of commentators, or the speculations of the Schoolmen. Some humanists, especially More, Erasmus, and Lily, wished to add spice and breadth to life by translating Greek drama, epigrams, and the dialogues of Lucian. Colet and Grocyn wrote and lectured on religion; Grocyn and Linacre helped More and others toward a mastery of Greek; Lily taught in the school Colet established at St. Paul's; Linacre published six Latin translations from Galen between 1517 and 1524, led in establishing a college of physicians, and founded lectureships in medicine at both universities. Erasmus improved his Greek and settled himself to the great work of his life: publishing accurate texts of scripture and of the writings by the fathers of the early church. Since he did not write or speak English, his translations were from Greek to Latin, and his original works were in Latin.

Translations of the Old Testament from Hebrew, of the New Testament from Greek, and of many other works (both religious and secular) from inaccurate and garbled Latin into fluent Renaissance Latin, or from Greek into Latin became extremely important. Of course earlier translators needed a sound knowledge of Hebrew or Greek or Latin—or all three. Later, translations from Greek and Latin into English increased in numbers. In the first part of the sixteenth century, a man who habitually read serious works could read Latin, and soon after 1500 women who were serious readers could usually do the same. The translations from the classics were a mere trickle at first, becoming a rivulet by midcentury, and later a river. In the latter part of the century translations from French, Italian, or Spanish made the river a flood. The emphasis in the education of both men and women was placed on the study of foreign languages. Women left translations of the classics as evidence of their skill and as contributions to the public.

During these developments in the early part of the sixteenth century, the main influence on the education of women was Sir Thomas More. Catherine of Aragon, with her thorough classical training in Spain, also contributed. But More had expressed in action his concern with teaching children Latin when he and John Holt published their Latin grammar, *Lac puerorum*, or *Milk for Babes*, by 1500, or earlier. They dedicated it to Cardinal Morton, who died in that year. Catherine came to England in 1501. More's discussion and the woodcuts emphasized the fact that the book was adapted to the tender minds of children. More's interest probably developed further through the education of his own children—Margaret, born in 1505, Elizabeth and Cecily in 1506 and 1507, and John in 1508 or 1509. Did the More children use *Lac puerorum*? And since Jerome, as well as classic writers, recommended that fathers, even those of high rank, do some teaching of their own children, did More follow the suggestion before he was drawn into affairs at court? Such questions are interesting, but they must remain speculations. Later, it is well known, More enlarged his school, with Margaret Gigs and Alice Middleton, foster daughter and stepdaughter, and with others outside the home—his niece, Frances Staverton; Anne Cresacre, who became his son's wife; perhaps Margaret Barrow, the wife of Thomas Elyot; and William Roper, who married Margaret More. The school was dominantly feminine, perhaps by accident, not design.

About 1518 More became the first Englishman to make a positive declaration in favor of a liberal education for women; he explained his view to William Gonell, a new teacher in his school. He valued even moderate learning in a woman, he said, above the riches of Croesus or the beauty of Helen, and the harvest was much the same whether a man or a woman did the sowing: "They both have the name of human being whose nature reason differentiates from beasts; both I say, are equally suited for the knowledge of learning by which reason is cultivated. . . ."

More's influence is further suggested by the fact that the other important defenders of a liberal education for women by 1540 were his friends and associates. Richard Herde, a tutor in his school, wrote an ardent defense about 1524, as an introduction to Margaret Roper's translation of the *Precatio dominica* by Erasmus. With the aid and approval of More, Herde also translated *De institutione Christianae foeminae* by Vives, dedicating his work to Catherine of Aragon. Vives, who was More's guest when in England, prepared *De ratione studii puerilis,* for girls, and *Satellitium animi sive symbola* in the same year, to help Catherine educate her daughter. Even Thomas Elyot, whose contacts with More may have begun as early as 1503 and were definite in the 1520s through their connection with the Council, gave belated and conventional support in his *Defense of Good Women,* 1540—when the women were queens, living in other countries.

More was a pioneer, at least among Englishmen, in emphasizing other principles of education besides the liberal education of women. They included the adapting of methods to young and tender minds; kindness and gentleness instead of scolding and beating; praise even for modest achievement when effort deserved it; piety and character, including humility, modesty, and self-control; the use of the best available teachers; and a sound training in the classics. Evidence appears in his letters to members of his school—letters easily available in the work of Elizabeth F. Rogers, in Hallett's translations of Stapleton's life of More, and in other biographies of More.

More's principles were used by many great teachers through the sixteenth century—those who praised women scholars or were praised by them—Sir Anthony Cooke, John Aylmer, Roger Ascham, Richard

Mulcaster—but these principles were not universally observed. Thomas Tusser complained in verse of the beatings he received from Nicholas Udall (a classical scholar). Roger Ascham's comments on the boys who had run away from school because they were beaten were followed by pleas for gentleness and for making learning attractive. Without the principles More emphasized it seems doubtful whether sixteenth-century women would have become famous for their classical learning.

More's position at court also gave him a chance to exert influence on the education of women. In October, 1517, he became a member of the Council, held other positions also, and from October, 1529, to May 16, 1532, he was lord chancellor. Unlike Erasmus, Richard Herde, Thomas Elyot, and other defenders of a liberal education, he could offer flesh and blood evidence of success by presenting his three daughters. About 1529 the daughters "disputed in philosophy" before the king—as John Palsgrave told us by his chance remark in a letter to More, when he regretted that he had not been present. Probably all those in attendance at court that day heard the disputation, and probably they reported the event in detail to many who were absent.

It is a fact that a number of men connected with the court when More was important there had daughters who later became classical scholars. Among them were Edward Seymour, Duke of Somerset and Protector; Henry Fitzalan, twelfth Earl of Arundel; and Henry Howard, Earl of Surrey. Seymour had been a page to the king's sister Mary when she went to marry the French king; had gone with the Duke of Suffolk to France in 1523 and had been knighted at Calais; and had become an esquire of the king's household in 1524. In the years that followed, his contact with the court continued. Henry Fitzalan was named for the king, who stood in person as godfather for him; at fifteen he chose to enter the king's service. For five or six years he had every chance to learn about the education of the More daughters. The Earl of Surrey came to court in 1529 to be a companion to the king's natural son, Henry Fitzroy, and to be educated with him. He held this position until 1533. In their classical achievements, the daughters these men produced compare favorably with the daughters of More and of Sir Anthony Cooke; their attainments will be discussed later in the chapter.

Some influence of Thomas More on the household school of Sir Humphrey Wingfield seems probable (as this writer suggested in *The Sir Thomas More Circle*)—the school where Roger Ascham had his early education in "the book and the bow." Of course the emphasis on archery owed nothing to More; and when Ascham said that Wingfield "ever loved and used to have many children brought up in learning in his house," *children* may have meant only boys. But contacts between More and Humphrey were certainly close; both were members of the Council, and in 1526 both were named on a small committee from that group to handle matters of law. Even if the school did not admit girls, More may have influenced Humphrey to accept principles of education that Ascham warmly defended later.

Probably More had little direct influence on the education of Mary Tudor, the daughter of Henry VIII. Catherine of Aragon, her mother, was fully capable of planning her education, and she seems to have done so, with the help of Vives and Linacre. But Garrett Mattingly told us that Catherine established a household school for the Princess Mary, bringing in daughters of the nobility and even persuading the king's sister Mary to resume her Latin. With his eyes on Spain as usual, Mattingly assumed that Catherine's pattern was the school established for her brother Juan in Spain some twenty-five years earlier. But More's dominantly feminine school was near in both time and place; his daughters, all born by 1507, would have been in school before 1516, when the Princess Mary was born. Also More and Catherine were friends; they had probably discussed his school more than once before she planned the education of her daughter. Thus her program may have been influenced in some details by the experience of More.

Probably More had no direct influence whatever on the education of the Princess Elizabeth. But Catherine Parr supervised much of her education; and since her sister Anne had written Roger Ascham that in her parental household education was based on that of the More family, there may have been indirect influence. More also had no direct influence on the views of William Cecil about the education of women, for in 1535, the year More was executed, Cecil was a schoolboy entering St. John's College; and though Cecil had married a classical scholar, he seemed comparatively unconcerned about the classical education of women. No direct contacts are apparent between More and Sir Henry Grey, the father of Lady Jane Grey, and from the present evidence, none between More and Sir Anthony Cooke, with his four daughters who were classical scholars.

Meantime, the ability to speak with correctness and even eloquence in classical Latin and to do so extempore had become important as the Renaissance developed on the Continent. In England also the ability to speak other foreign languages, as well as Latin, was being suggested. Henry VII, no classical scholar himself, found it advisable to send to the papal and the secular courts men who spoke Latin well. The prestige of England suffered if an Englishman faltered or sat down without finishing his oration or if unfriendly listeners found flaws in his structure or diction. Lacking competent Englishmen at first, Henry used or imported such men as Pietro Carmeliano, Adrian de Castello, Giovanni Gigli, and Silvestro Gigli, rewarding them with ecclesiastical positions, even bishoprics. Later, when men like More and Lily were available, Henry did not use them. Perhaps, as William Nelson suggested, he distrusted satirical and imaginative young men who were translating semi-bawdy Greek epigrams and turning Lucian into Latin.

To help schoolboys in learning to speak Latin fluently, instead of merely reading it or translating it, was one of the aims of Erasmus in writing his *Colloquies*. In discussing this aim Craig R. Thompson said that Latin in the period "was still an eminently practical subject, the key to careers in the church, law, medicine, and other professions, besides being the medium of much contemporary scholarship." An Englishman who wished learned men on the Continent to read his work chose Latin, as Sir Thomas More did in writing *Utopia*.

Writers on the teaching of the classics also emphasized the importance of speaking Latin. Although More did not stress it in the letters to his school, he was fluent enough himself to discuss extempore in Latin important details of trade or other diplomatic affairs. Vives suggested that children use first their native language and then move gradually, under the supervision of a teacher, to good Latin: "By the gradual increase of knowledge, at last they will become Latin conversationalists." In the first book and fifth chapter of the *Governour*, Sir Thomas Elyot said that children might begin by learning the Latin names of all things in sight and of all parts of their bodies and that it would be best for a nobleman's son to have with him continually only those who would help him speak "pure and elegant Latin." Ascham warned against letting children try to speak Latin before they were ready to speak correctly, but added, "Yet all men covet to have their children speak Latin, and so do I, very earnestly too."

Perhaps the most surprising emphasis on speaking the learned languages appears in the statutes planned for St. John's College, Cambridge, by Bishop Fisher, under the influence of Erasmus. They provided not only for the teaching of Hebrew as well as Greek and Latin,

but as J. K. McConica commented, "both versions [1516, 1524] antici-
pate ordinary conversations within the college in Latin, Greek, or
Hebrew." As the statutes of St. John's are said to be almost identical
with the ones planned earlier for Christ's College, probably both institutions put the same emphasis upon the speaking of all three languages. Whether ordinary conversations were ever carried on in Hebrew is another question—but at least they were the ideal.

    With this emphasis upon the classics and upon the speaking
of Latin in the education of men, it should not seem strange that the
outstanding development in the education of women during the sixteenth century was a sound classical education. Such an education
meant the ability to read Latin and Greek books easily, almost as
easily as if they were English, and to know something about the lives
and the times, as well as the ideas of classical writers. It meant skill
in translating from Greek into Latin or from either of them into English. It meant the ability to compose orations, declamations, or personal letters in fluent and correct Latin by the standards of the
Renaissance, to carry on a correspondence with famous theologians on
the Continent, or even to write epitaphs in Latin or Greek verse. It
meant the ability to speak extempore in Latin with fluency on informal or formal occasions.

    A few women also had the ability to speak Greek well. Two
of them were Lady Burghley and Lady Jane Grey. In a letter to
Sturm, December, 1550, Roger Ascham said that the skill of Lady
Jane, both in writing and in speaking Greek, was almost incredible.
As he made the comments in private letters to a friend on the Continent, he could hardly have expected to gain favor by his remarks.
Ascham did not hesitate to say, also in private letters, that Queen
Elizabeth spoke Greek only moderately well, although she conversed
very well when she spoke Latin with him. When Richard Mulcaster
was praising the ability of women trained in the classics to speak
the languages, he said that any man who doubted their ability should
begin a conversation with them in one of these languages, presumably
meaning Greek or Latin. Thus we need not depend entirely upon
Ascham for evidence of their ability to speak both languages.

    Some modern students of the Renaissance are inclined to dis-
miss the sound classical learning of Tudor women as mere decoration

based on egotism. But to most of the women, with a few exceptions, Latin especially had serious uses, as it had to men of the period. To deal first with generalities and later with specifics, it probably gave many women a sense of achievement, a feeling that seems to rank higher than cherishing an empty head. Those who spoke Latin easily must have had a oneness with their times and an intellectual equality with their husbands and their husbands' guests. Since English was not a language used in sixteenth-century diplomacy and since the English never expected people from other countries to speak English, women like Lady Burghley, who were hostesses in great houses to important guests, had a real asset, it seems, when they could speak Latin in social conversation.

Throughout the Tudor Age women who had skill in classical and in other foreign languages used them for various purposes they considered worthy. Margaret Beaufort, who knew little Latin and less Greek but had some command of French, translated *The Mirror of Gold for the Sinful Soul* and one book of the *Imitation of Christ,* to further religious devotion. Lady Mary Sidney, wife of Sir Henry Sidney, knew Italian well enough to use it at times when she acted as an intermediary for the queen in 1559 about a possible marriage to the Archduke Charles. The unnamed women mentioned by Nicholas Udall in prefatory remarks for the *Paraphrase* by Erasmus, and by William Harrison in his *Description of England,* suggest that a great number were putting their skill in languages to good use. Anne Locke, mentioned in Chapter 7 of this work, and many others were using their knowledge to further their religious beliefs. They were not egotists displaying a mere ornament.

Thomas More certainly did not regard the sound classical education he gave his daughters as an ornament. In letters to members of his school, he emphasized piety and humility, not pride, and he wrote to his daughter Margaret that her home would give her scope for all her talents and that he did not wish to see her enter public life. Probably he would have agreed with the ideas of Erasmus in his *Colloquies*—that a sound classical education would give a woman the wisdom to be a better wife, and mother and would contribute to a more permanent and a happier union. Or he may have given some of these ideas to Erasmus!

When Margaret More Roper suggested an emendation in the text of Saint Cyprian, one that Erasmus accepted and used in his edition of that holy father's work, and when she translated into English the *Precatio dominica* of Erasmus, she was not feeding her ego but making a contribution to religion for others. Perhaps she would have done more with her scholarship if the execution of her father had not filled her life with grief and if religious changes and the need for self-effacement for fear of danger to her and her family had not existed. But she educated her daughters as she and her sisters had been educated. One daughter, Mary Bassett, perhaps translated into English the *Ecclesiastical History* of Eusebius (though some believe that Margaret herself did the work); but it was certainly Mary who turned into English the part of More's *Treatise on the Passion* that he had written in Latin. She was able to follow with fidelity the spirit and the style of More, it is said, and her English version was included in the 1557 edition of More's *Works*.

The three learned daughters of Edward Seymour, Duke of Somerset and Protector (a man who had been for some years at court with More), also did not use their skill in languages as a mere ornament. For three years Thomas Cranmer was their tutor, it is said, and for another three years Nicholas Denisot, who seems to have given them his own appreciation for Margaret of Navarre. According to reports about them, they had great facility "in reading and writing, even apparently in speaking both Latin and Greek. . . ." One daughter, Jane, by 1549 was corresponding in Latin with religious reformers on the Continent: Martin Bucer and also Fagius, as he was often called, though his name was Paul Büchlin.

But the special achievement of all three Seymour sisters was the composing of a hundred Latin distichs or couplets to honor Margaret of Navarre at her death, in 1549. Their work was published by Denisot, who had become one of the literary men connected with the court of Margaret. The next year their work appeared again with a French title page. Denisot's introduction described the couplets as divine poems by three divine and learned sisters who honored the queen, not for her rank but for her piety and her learning. The volume contained an address to the three young poets written by Nicholas de Herberay, the translator of *Amadis de Gaul,* and an ode by Ronsard, praising the sisters and the literary union of France and England they had helped to achieve.

The two daughters of Henry Fitzalan, twelfth Earl of Arundel (another man who had been at court with Sir Thomas More), used their education in quiet ways that perhaps seemed important to them. Their father educated his daughters at home along with his stepson. As Arundel was a powerful leader of the Catholic nobility, Queen

Elizabeth restored him to his position as lord high steward and in 1559 appointed him chancellor of Oxford University. When he resigned his position as chancellor a few months later, he brought home with him a young man named Humphrey Lloyd, who helped him to continue the building of his library. His daughters, Mary and Jane, had a wide influence on his library. For them he acquired many books on music and also many Greek and Latin volumes.

Each daughter made translations but left them in manuscript instead of publishing them. Mary, who became the wife of the Duke of Norfolk, died about a year later, probably in childbirth, when she was about sixteen. She left with her father four volumes of manuscripts she had translated from Greek into Latin. These became a part of his library, later called the Lumley Library. Jane Fitzalan had married Lord Lumley, and after the death of Mary, Arundel invited him and his wife to move permanently from Durham to Nonsuch Castle, making their home with him. As a result, Jane spent most of her married life in her father's house, and her books and manuscripts became part of the Arundel-Lumley collection. Her manuscripts included the orations of Isocrates to Nicocles, dedicated to her father, and other orations of Isocrates, all of them having been translated from Greek into Latin. She left a manuscript copy of *Iphigenia* also, one that she had translated from Greek into English.

The three daughters of Henry Howard, Earl of Surrey (and Surrey also had been at court with Thomas More from 1529 to More's resignation in 1532) had a classical education. When Surrey's children were ready for their education, he secured John Foxe, the martyrologist, as a tutor for both sons and daughters, giving them the same chance at Latin and Greek. When William Barker composed *The Nobility of Women*, perhaps about 1559, he praised Jane especially. He said that she had "such marvelous towardness in learning as few men may compare with her. Both Greek and Latin is vulgar—her composition in verses so notable that all the world doth acknowledge her a worthy daughter of a most worthy father." When he said that both languages were vulgar to her, probably he meant that she used them as if they were native tongues. No tangible evidence of her skill remains; and we have no way of judging whether her learning merely fostered her ego or whether she used it for a purpose she considered worthy. Barker's work, with its praise of many women, does suggest that it had become fashionable by this time in the century to praise women for their classical achievements, and that he was less concerned with the question whether they used it for the good of others.

Though the father of Lady Jane Grey seemed to have no apparent association with Sir Thomas More, her classical learning was prodigious for a young woman of her age. It included a skill in speaking Greek that Roger Ascham described as incredible, and since he once wrote that Queen Elizabeth spoke Greek only moderately well, one may be the more inclined to believe him. She used her education as a solace and an escape from impossible parents. When Roger Ascham stopped to see her in 1550 at Bradgate, she spoke frankly about the difference between her parents and her teacher, John Aylmer, a difference she considered one of her greatest benefits from God. Her parents expected perfection from her in every movement and gesture, and when she failed to attain it, she was taunted, threatened, given bobs, pinches, and other punishments she would not name because she honored her parents. "I think myself in hell," she said, until the time came for her to report to Master Aylmer. He taught her gently, using "such fair allurements to learning that I think all the time nothing while I am with him. And when I am called from him, I fall on weeping, because whatsoever I do else but learning is full of grief, trouble, fear, and whole misliking unto me." Since there is some evidence that Lady Jane was cursed by her father and beaten by her mother until she agreed to marry Guildford Dudley, after her first positive refusal, probably Ascham's account of his talk with her was reasonably accurate. Lady Jane also used her Latin in correspondence with Heinrich Bullinger, a learned and tolerant pastor at Zurich, and with some other Calvinist and Zwinglian ministers on the Continent, including John Ulmis and Martin Bucer. In one source it is suggested that she made contact with them through her tutors; in another, that they were writing her father. As he was often busy or away from home, she began answering for him. But no matter how it began, the letters remain—the originals in the library at Zurich and the printed versions in *Original Letters* by the Parker Society. As Lady Jane was only sixteen or seventeen years old when she was executed because of her father's plotting, it is impossible to estimate what she would have done with her classical education if she had lived a life of normal length.

Although later writers tended to say that Sir Anthony Cooke followed the educational theories of Sir Thomas More, there seems to be no evidence of direct association. But four daughters of Cooke were given a sound classical education. A fifth daughter, Margaret, married Ralph Rowlett in the summer of 1558, probably while her father was still in exile, but died a few weeks later. We know nothing of her classical education. Mildred Cooke, perhaps the oldest daughter of the family, married William Cecil, the great statesman, and eventually became Lady Burghley. She published no books or translations but not from lack of classical learning, since it is said that she spoke Greek almost as easily as she spoke English. She made her contribution to England as a hostess to leading statesmen from other countries and as a politically minded wife who understood and aided her husband. She had translated St. Chrysostom, but when she learned that another scholar had done the same work, she refused to publish her translation. Thus she indicated (to this writer, at least) that she was a modest woman who did not make a display of her learning; and competent historians, in writing biographies of her husband, have also emphasized her modesty. If she spoke Greek fluently, she probably conversed in Latin easily, since the latter skill was usually developed by a man or a woman with a sound classical education. When a Spanish diplomat, for example, reported to his government the details of his talk with her about the marriage of Queen Elizabeth, one might suppose that the two had been speaking Latin. Thus Lady Burghley may have found classical learning useful in daily life, since English was not a language of diplomacy and since she was often a hostess to diplomats and other important visitors from the Continent.

Anne Cooke Bacon (sister of Lady Burghley, wife of Sir Nicholas Bacon, the keeper of the great seal, and mother of Sir Francis Bacon), proved to her own satisfaction that she could use her knowledge of Italian for worthy purposes when she translated and published twelve sermons by Bernardine Ochino into English about 1550 and twenty-five sermons from the same preacher in 1570. A modest dedication to her mother, Anne Fitzwilliam, as the Lady F, described the sermons as treating of "the election and predestination of God" and as proceeding from the "happy spirit of the sanctified Bernardine." Apparently her mother had once doubted whether her study of Italian was worthwhile, but she felt that in these translations she was proving her ability to use the language for religious purposes and the glory of God. Probably her use of her classical education to further religion gave her even greater satisfaction when she translated Bishop Jewel's *Apology in Defense of the Church of England* from Latin to English. He had written his Latin version for people on the Continent; her translation was for people in England who did not read Latin. She sent one copy of her translation to the author with a letter in Greek, perhaps complimenting him rather than exalting herself, and he replied with a letter in the same language. She sent another copy of her complete translation to Archbishop Parker. Both men accepted her work without the change of a single word; thus she proved her knowledge of theology, it seems, as well as Latin. A first copy was quickly returned to her in print; a second issue carried a dedication to her. Many of her letters, when they were written to people who understood the classical languages, were peppered with Greek and Latin quotations, not because she wished to display her knowledge but because she thought easily and communicated well in those languages. She also corresponded in Latin with Theodore Beza, the famous theologian who succeeded Calvin at Geneva. He honored her by dedicating to her *Christian Meditations upon Eight Psalms,* published in an English translation of 1582. He paid tribute to her Christian courage, like that of her father, he said, and her knowledge of the great and holy doctors, both Latin and Greek.

Lady Elizabeth Russell, perhaps the third daughter of Sir Anthony Cooke and his wife, had skill in using both Latin and Greek. She seemed to specialize in epitaphs. She composed a Greek quatrain and a six-line poem in Latin, to be used for her sister Catherine in the London church where she was buried; a Latin epitaph for a Thomas Noke in Berkshire; Latin epitaphs for her first husband, Sir Thomas Hoby, and for his half-brother, Sir Philip Hoby, at Bisham; verses in English, Latin, and Greek for her second husband, John, Lord Russell, in Wesminster Abbey; and inscriptions in both Latin and Greek for herself and her daughters who had died, to use with the monument she planned for herself at Bisham. In these she tended to center on herself and members of her family. In 1605 she published her translation from Latin into English of *A Way of Reconciliation . . . Touching the True Nature and Substance of the Body and Blood of Christ.* Judging from the title, one might think that she was expressing religious views she considered important, or even trying to aid King James in uniting the Anglican and the Catholic churches. But the dedication reveals her as a self-centered woman, chiefly concerned with the social status of herself and her daughter, and with the possibility that the daughter might become a countess.

Catherine, probably the fourth daughter of Sir Anthony Cooke and his wife, judging from her marriage in 1565 and the birth dates of several children, was the wife of Henry Killigrew. He was a friend of William Cecil and an outstanding diplomat, who served the queen almost to the end of her reign. Catherine was praised for her proficiency in Latin, Greek, and Hebrew, as well as her skill in composing verses. She did not leave overwhelming evidence of her ability to use these languages, though she once addressed some Latin verses to her sister Mildred and used one Greek word in another Latin quatrain. The quatrain, expressing her faith in the resurrection, was used on her monument in the London church where she was buried. Many verses from others appear there also, giving her extravagant praise for her knowledge of languages and illustrating again the tendency through much of the sixteenth century to praise women for being classical scholars. Aside from the question of languages, she did have the courage while she lived to befriend the fiery nonconformist preacher, Edward Dering, and to support her husband and other members of the Council who refused to stop his public lectures.

Queens who shared the throne with kings and those who ruled in their own right, as well as commoners, often found a thorough classical education and a knowledge of other foreign languages useful in their daily lives.

One of these queens was Catherine of Aragon. In Spain her mother had provided for her a sound classical education, securing the best available teachers; some of the teachers were women who became lecturers at the universities in Spain. With that education she was able to build her own library and, after she became queen, she made it available to English scholars. She was a friend of Richard Whitford at Sion House, and her frequent visits there probably encouraged his devotional writing. Apparently John Leland, who became a famous antiquarian later, used her library freely, both at Greenwich and at Richmond. When William Blount, Lord Mountjoy, was the only nobleman genuinely interested in scholarship, she appointed him as her chamberlain. Garrett Mattingly, in *Catherine of Aragon,* suggests that she probably furthered appointments for Thomas Linacre, John Colet, Thomas More, and Richard Pace. She befriended and encouraged Erasmus and Vives; among other actions she urged More to translate or to arrange for another to translate into English the work known as *The Instruction of a Christian Woman.* Richard Herde, a tutor at one time in More's household school, translated the work, dedicating it to Queen Catherine. When Wolsey and the queen were not on good terms about other affairs, she continued to approve of his suppressing decayed religious houses and using the funds from them to endow his new colleges at Ipswich and at Oxford. She contributed to lectureships and supported poor scholars at both universities, taking a personal interest in the progress of these scholars.

She planned the education of her daughter Mary, with the help of Linacre and Vives, and perhaps with some inspiration from More's school. She also enlarged the school to include some older women of the court, one of them being the king's younger sister Mary.

Without her early classical education it seems that Catherine would have been unable to do any of these things. Without that education, giving her a world of abstract ideas, it also seems probable that she would have been unable to encourage her husband in the early years of his rule or to succeed as regent while he was in France. And without the knowledge of law, including canon law, included in that education, perhaps she would have been unable to think and act with courage in the solitary years from 1532 to 1536, or to resist starting a civil war for herself or for her daughter.

Catherine Parr was another queen who apparently found Latin and other foreign languages useful when she shared a throne. Her knowledge of Latin was probably greater than most scholars assume that it was. Her sister Anne received Latin letters from Roger Ascham, lent him a Latin volume of Cicero, and told him in one letter that the education her parents planned for their children was modeled on that of the Thomas More household. It would be something of a feat to follow More's plan and to give little or no attention to Latin! It is true that the nine-year-old Prince Edward wrote her a letter in 1546 congratulating her on her progress in "Latina lingua et bonis literis." But though G. Fenno Hoffman, Jr., offered it as evidence that Catherine had not learned Latin early in life, such a conclusion seems doubtful. Probably the little boy did not fully grasp the nature of her involvement, and she may have been mentioning her own use of Latin to encourage him. It seems also that some knowledge of Latin would be almost essential to her work of supervising the *Paraphrase* by Erasmus, even though she had a competent general editor in Nicholas Udall. Also for two books of the work, Matthew and the Acts, the name of the translator is never given. Though there is no definite evidence, the lack of information suggests the possibility that Catherine may have translated them herself and was too modest or too much inclined to fear the disapproval of Henry VIII to reveal her part in it. At least she did not publish the work while he was living.

Whether Catherine could have successfully reorganized the royal school and supervised the education of Elizabeth and Edward without a knowledge of Latin, as well as other languages, seems doubtful. Edward wrote her a number of letters in Latin, sometimes assuring her that he was striving for improvement before writing her further. Without the ability to read them or to make suggestions on them, it seems that she would have been in an embarrassing position. Besides owning an Italian copy of Petrarch, published in Venice in 1534, a copy that bears her arms, she received a letter in Italian from the Princess Elizabeth. The manuscript copies of the letter Catherine wrote to the Princess Mary, urging her to publish the gospel of John she had translated and to use her name with it, are in Latin; it seems unlikely that anyone else would have taken the trouble to translate them from English into Latin. She also wrote one devotional poem in French, it is said. These facts apparently suggest a working knowledge of several foreign languages, including Latin.

Another question is what language Catherine Parr used when she talked with foreign ambassadors or other important visitors who came to the court while she was queen. She took the initiative in meeting and speaking at some length with the Duke of Nájera and also with Chapuys. Since English was not the language of diplomacy, perhaps they used French or more likely Latin, the latter language being a means of international communication. Whatever else may be true, Catherine Parr seems to have used languages but not to have paraded her learning.

Queen Elizabeth found many uses for classical and other foreign languages in her work of governing England, valuing especially, it seems, her ability to speak them fluently. Though her oratory and her political ideas may have been influenced by a study of Isocrates, she had the good judgment not to quote at length from the classics or the Bible but to speak with simplicity and power and to stress the emotions she and her people shared. At times of crisis her orations made an important contribution to her ability to govern.

When she visited the universities she often needed to speak Latin or Greek. In 1564 she answered a speaker at the University of Cambridge in Latin after she had been warned by Cecil that she must not respond in English. In 1566 at Oxford when a professor gave her an official welcome in Greek, she thanked him in Greek. But her response was brief, perhaps conventional, and may have been memorized, thus agreeing with the statement made once by Roger Ascham that she spoke Greek only "moderately well." In 1592 on another visit to Oxford, she gave an address in Latin on the need to honor all law, both human and divine.

Perhaps the queen valued most highly her ability to speak languages when she was dealing with foreign ambassadors and could dispense with interpreters. In a single day, Roger Ascham reported, he had heard her answer one ambassador in Italian, one in French, and one in Latin, "Not haltingly [but] promptly, without discomposure. . . ." Other evidence also supports the fact that she had the ability to do so. In 1597 her entire court listened to the extempore tongue-lashing in Latin that she gave a Polish ambassador. As his father had been friendly to England and as she understood that he had come to seek peace, she received him in the presence chamber and in open court. But after a formal greeting he drew back and began making threats, with a face like a storm cloud. Rising from her throne, Queen Elizabeth told him in forceful Latin that if he came from a king, that king must be new and not of royal blood. As for himself, he had perhaps read many books without finding what he needed to know—the courteous terms to be used between kings and princes. Apparently the court wanted to applaud, delighted with their queen.

The learned languages, intellectual pursuits, and solid reading at hand—all aided the queen in keeping an orderly court, according to William Harrison in *The Description of England*, with his account of the court:

And to say how many gentlemen and ladies there are, that beside sound knowledge of the Greek and Latin tongues, are therefore no less skillful in the Spanish, Italian, and French, or in some one of them, it resteth not in me, sith I am persuaded that as the noblemen and gentlemen do surmount in this behalf, so these [the ladies] come very little or nothing at all behind them for their parts; which industry God continue. . . .

Besides these things, I could in like sort set down the ways and means whereby our ancient ladies of the court do shun and avoid idleness . . . some in continual reading either of the Holy Scriptures, or histories of our own or foreign nations about us, and divers in writing volumes of their own, or translating other men's into our English and Latin tongue. . . .

As a result, the shocking behavior disgracing many foreign courts was either banished completely from the court of Elizabeth, Harrison said, or kept under control by her officers. Another means of preventing trouble was to furnish solid reading:

Finally to avoid idleness and prevent sundry transgressions . . . every office hath either a Bible or the books of *The Acts and Monuments of the Church of England*, or both, besides some histories and chronicles . . . whereby the stranger that entereth . . . on the sudden shall rather imagine himself to come into some public school of the universities, where many give ear to one that readeth, than into a prince's palace, if you confer the same with other nations.

Even if Harrison's account suffered no diminishing in the telling, it helps us to understand the learned and intellectual women and the respect they were given in much of the sixteenth century.

But as the century was drawing to a close, enthusiasm about classical learning or any literary education for women was waning. Probable causes for the decline were numerous. Faith in the classics as a means of improving English life had lessened. The Bible had been made available in English, and perhaps the growth of Puritanism had created a demand for religious books instead of secular reading. For those who read the classics, many translations into French and from French into English were available. Also secular literature by English writers in the English language had grown in volume and in variety. Though the change was beginning before the death of Elizabeth, probably the accession of King James, with his hostility to learned women and his frivolous queen, hurried it.

It is significant, perhaps, that the term bluestocking, applied with a derogatory suggestion to a woman of intellectual and literary interests, did not appear for nearly a hundred and fifty years after the death of Queen Elizabeth. Though a modern translator of a Spanish diplomat's report on Mildred Cecil used the word of her, his use was an anachronism. The term, according to the *New English Dictionary,* was used for the first time in 1653, but only for those men who were members of the Little Parliament, because of their mean and plain attire. It was first applied to women about 1750 to 1757, when those who attended Mrs. Montagu's assemblies earned the title by refusing to wear formal dress. All these derogatory uses, for men or women, were associated with the clothing they wore; they did not suggest contempt for learning. In the sixteenth century many women famous for a classical education dressed magnificently—Catherine of Aragon on formal occasions as queen; Mildred, Lady Burghley, as the wife and hostess of the leading statesman; Catherine Parr while she was the wife of Henry VIII; and Queen Elizabeth. And through most of the sixteenth century women were honored for their classical learning.

Signs of change began appearing by 1589, when the author of *The Art of English Poesy* said that he was writing "for the learning of ladies or young gentlemen or idle courtiers . . . since to such . . . minds nothing is more cumbersome than tedious doctrines and scholarly methods of discipline."

In 1598 determined opposition to any liberal education for women appeared as *The Necessary, Fit, and Convenient Education of a Young Gentlewoman,* an English translation from an Italian work by Bruto. The author insisted that it was not "convenient" to educate a girl in the humane arts and sciences. Only a gentlewoman of a noble house should speak Latin. Woman was given to man to help him; she should not govern estates and commonwealths nor prescribe laws for men. She might be allowed to read Plutarch, scripture, and accounts of other women who loved their countries and their husbands.

About 1600 many parents preferred to have their daughters innocent of classical languages or any foreign language. Lady Anne Clifford, born in 1590, studied no language except English because her father would not allow it. She read widely in English literature and in translations—Epictetus, Boethius, Saint Augustine, the history of the church by Eusebius, Ovid, *Don Quixote,* Spenser, and the prose and poetry of Samuel Daniel, her tutor. If she had been born a half century earlier, she would probably have studied both Greek and Latin.

Mrs. Lucy Apsley Hutchinson, born in 1620, told of her education in a brief autobiography. She learned French and English together; and when she was about seven, she had eight tutors for these languages, and for music, dancing, writing, and needlework. She liked Latin, and with only the help of the family chaplain, surpassed her brothers who were away at school. Though her father was tolerant about her study of Latin, her mother feared she would injure her health with study and disliked having a daughter who preferred Latin to other things.

During the one hundred eighteen years from the accession of Henry VII in 1485 to the death of Elizabeth in 1603, women with an intellectual drive, and usually with a sound classical education as well, were great influences at the English court: Margaret Beaufort, the king's beloved mother, 1485–1509; Catherine of Aragon, queen without question, 1509–1527, and nominal queen until 1532; Catherine

Parr, sharing the throne of Henry VIII, 1543–1547; Queen Mary, ruling in her own right, 1553–1558; and Queen Elizabeth, also ruling in her own right, 1558–1603. These women, influential for a hundred years of the Tudor Age, must have encouraged other women with scholarly interests to feel at home in the court and to pursue intellectual affairs.

The participation of many women in business had ended about 1500. But a few women continued to manage businesses of some size through the sixteenth and seventeenth centuries. By the middle of the seventeenth century, men were ceasing to name their wives as executors of great estates. The approval of a sound classical education for women or the praise of women for studying liberal subjects was dwindling away about 1600. A few women of intellectual ambition, like Margaret, Duchess of Newcastle, and a few who were learned in languages, like Bathsua Makin, appeared in the seventeenth century. Though other factors were doubtless involved, James I, the Cromwells, and Charles II did not encourage the development of intellectual women. By the Restoration in 1660, women of rank and fashion were becoming idle and frivolous, and, it seems, were being imitated by women of lesser status.

Women as Literary Patrons and as Writers

W H E N Caxton set up his printing press at Westminster in 1476, he laid the foundation for a broad literary patronage with the help of Earl Rivers, other noblemen, Margaret Beaufort, and even wealthy citizens of London. Earlier, writers had usually been supported by monasteries to which they belonged, by the king, or by other noblemen in their great houses. A few, like Chaucer, held a job and did their writing in their spare time. When printed copies became available at comparatively low prices, the number of readers and buyers increased but not rapidly enough to assure profits to an author. As late as 1600, the writer of a pamphlet who received forty shillings for an outright sale was lucky; and it was late in the seventeenth century before John Dryden, for example, made a contract with his bookseller, Tonson, promising him more money than he might expect from any patron. Hence, throughout the Tudor period, literary patrons were important, and many of them were women.

Certain facts about patronage, already well established, may serve as background without detailed support. Most books, through the Tudor period and beyond, had dedications, and about ninety percent of them, it has been estimated, were addressed to one or more patrons with hope of a reward. Many dedications were unauthorized, and some so-called writers were complete strangers to the persons they addressed. Thus a dedication might be an unhappy surprise. Other dedications expressed gratitude for past favors, with or without a glimmer of hope for possible future favors; and sometimes past favors were named with thanks that seemed heartfelt. The greater the writer, or the more widespread his reputation, the more he tended to dedicate to friends or acquaintances, and the more dignified his wording. Unestablished or mediocre writers, hoping to support themselves by their pens, sometimes used effusive flattery. When Thomas Nash addressed a different patron for each book he published, except for two aimed at the Careys, and when Robert Greene dedicated seventeen books to sixteen different people, perhaps each was trying for rewards with little success.

Writers without friends able to reward them might try to select a possible patron by estimating the official position, rank, wealth, special interests, and even the number of library books a man or woman owned. Any person who held high office in the government or was well known and favorably regarded for other reasons was likely to have many dedications. Lord Burghley received about a hundred—histories, books dealing with problems of state, many polemics against the Catholics—but almost no poetical or imaginative works. The Earl of Leicester acquired nearly as many; Eleanor Rosenberg listed 94 dedications for him. Sir Philip Sidney, popular as a person and a writer himself, received dedications in many books on various subjects during his short life. Queen Elizabeth, according to H. S. Bennett, had about 200 books and 50 manuscripts dedicated to her.

Among the women patrons of printed books in the sixteenth century, Margaret Beaufort, mother of Henry VII, was easily first in time and by no means last in importance. She encouraged three printers, Caxton, Wynkyn de Worde, and Pynson, asking them to print certain books and sometimes paying the cost of publication. Among the books she asked to have published were *A Treatise Concerning the Fruitful Sayings of David, King and Prophet* (seven sermons by Bishop Fisher), the *Sermon for Henry VII*, the *Brevarium . . . Hereford,* the *Brevarium . . . Sarum,* and *The Fifteen Oes.* This last one, acording to Henry R. Plomer, she commissioned Caxton to publish at her expense. The *Scala Prefectionis* was issued with a two-stanza l'envoi telling the reader that the author was Walter Hilton, that it was printed by Wynkyn de Worde in the house of Caxton, and that the mother of the king had directed him to publish the book for her. The Lady Margaret asked William Atkinson to translate from Latin to English the first three books of *The Imitation of Christ,* as she did not have the classical background for translating from Latin. She translated the fourth book of the same work from French into English. At her command, Wynkyn de Worde published the English version of all four books.

Religious as she was, the Lady Margaret concerned herself also with some secular material. In 1489 Caxton published *Blanchardine and Eglantine* with a dedication to her. He had sold her a French copy, she had returned it to him, he said; and at her request, "which I repute as for a commandment," he had turned it into English. The other secular book was *The Great Ship of Fools of this World*, which Henry Watson translated into English from French at the request of his master, Wynkyn de Worde, but "through the enticement and exhortation of the excellent Princess Margaret." Through these requests, some payments for publication, and her own translations (including *The Mirror of Gold for the Sinful Soul*), the Lady Margaret was apparently the first outstanding woman patron of books and of publishing.

Through the sixteenth century nearly every woman connected with royalty and many women of the aristocracy received one or more dedications. Of the queens of Henry VIII, Catherine of Aragon had five or six dedications; Anne Boleyn, two; Jane Seymour, none; Catherine Howard, one; Anne of Cleves, two, and also an early edition of Elyot's *Defense of Good Women;* and Catherine Parr, two, the first part of the translation of the *Paraphrase* by Erasmus and a religious work by Sir Anthony Cope. Though it seems unnecessary to name all the women who received dedications, they included Lady Elizabeth Russell, Lady Anne Bacon, Lady Burghley, and Catherine, Duchess of Suffolk. For others not named here see *The Index of Dedications,* by Franklin B. Williams, Jr.

Among the other women known as patrons were Bridget, the wife of Francis, Earl of Bedford; Margaret Russell Clifford, Countess of Cumberland; her daughter, Lady Anne Clifford, later Countess of Dorset, and later still, Countess of Montgomery and of Pembroke. Dedications to the Countess of Cumberland included the usual sermons and religious books; in 1596 she received a joint dedication with the Countess of Warwick of Spenser's *Four Hymns;* in 1599 Samuel Daniel addressed to her *A Letter from Octavia to Marcus Antonius,* and in 1603, one of the letters in *Certain Epistles.* Three of the *Epistles* he dedicated to men—Sir Thomas Egerton, Thomas, Lord Howard, and the Earl of Southampton; the other two he addressed to Lucy, Countess of Bedford, and to Lady Anne Clifford. As Daniel had been the tutor of Lady Anne and she had later erected a memorial expressing her gratitude to him, his dedications to her and her mother seem natural. Lady Anne received another dedication with *An April Shower,* from Henry Peacham, the Younger; it was written on the death of her first husband, the Earl of Dorset. About 1614–1616 Joshua Sylvester named her as one of several to whom he dedicated *The Parliament of Virtues* and also *The Second Session of the Parliament.* We do not have direct evidence about gifts to these writers; but considering the rank, the reputation, and the tastes of the people concerned (both those who gave and those who received) it seems probable that many of the dedications either expressed gratitude for past favors or led to future favors.

The three daughters of John Spencer of Althorp had dedications from Edmund Spenser because they were distant relatives, and apparently they responded with gifts. In 1590 Spenser honored Lady Elizabeth Carey, one of these daughters, with the sixteenth of the seventeen sonnets he published with the first three books of the *Faerie Queene.* A few months later he dedicated to her *Muiopotmos, or The Fate of the Butterfly,* mentioning "the excellent favors" he had received and praising her great bounty. Lady Elizabeth Carey was honored with other dedications: one from Thomas Churchyard, one from at least another writer on religion, and a flowery effusion from Thomas Nash; her daughter, also Elizabeth Carey, who became Lady Berkeley, had other dedications.

Spenser dedicated "The Tears of the Muses," published in *Complaints,* 1591, to another daughter of John Spencer, Lady Alice Strange. Her husband, Lord Strange (who succeeded his father as the Earl of Derby in 1593 but died the next year) was an amateur poet, the friend and patron of well-known dramatists and poets, and the protector of a group of players known as Lord Strange's Men. Spenser wished to honor Lady Strange, he said, for her "particular bounties," and for the "bands of affinity" between them that she had been pleased to acknowledge. By 1600 she had married Sir Thomas Egerton, Lord Chancellor Ellesmere, who was also a recognized patron of literary men.

In 1591 Spenser dedicated *Mother Hubbard's Tale* to Lady Compton and Mounteagle. She was Anne, the third daughter of John Spencer of Althorp. In his dedication Spenser mentioned the "humble affection and faithful duty which I have always professed and am bound to bear to that house from which you spring," but he did not thank her for favors. However, one of Spenser's biographers,

Alexander C. Judson, believes that she was probably the "bountiful Charillis" of *Colin Clout's Come Home Again,* in 1595. So two daughters of John Spencer of Althorp were certainly benefactors of Edmund Spenser, the third may have rewarded him for a dedication, and the first two were patrons of other literary men.

Queen Elizabeth was not a generous giver of patronage to literary men. Perhaps she never gave an author a reward that he considered adequate. About 1575 or 1576 George Gascoigne was a petitioner, with his "Tale of Hemetes the Heremyte"; but though he expressed gratitude later to her for rewards beyond his deserving, there is little evidence of a tangible gift. Roger Ascham once thanked the queen for her "bountiful goodness" in delivering him from legal troubles and other difficulties, but the year before he died (according to Lawrence V. Ryan) he was petitioning her for enough money so that he might leave something to his sons. Even in this situation Cecil had to take the initiative by reminding her of their needs. About 1580 Christopher Ocland, author of *Anglorum praelia,* a work that the queen and her Council had approved for the use of every school in the realm, was appealing to Sir Julius Caesar, master of requests, and about ten years later to Burghley, for relief from poverty and debt. John Lyly, who had published *Euphues* in 1578, and who continued from about 1584 to write plays for the court, had hoped for an appointment as Master of the Revels. In a second petition he spoke of thirteen years spent, a thousand hopes, and a hundred promises, and still he had nothing. Perhaps he was given to understand that he would have the position when it became vacant, but Lyly died in 1606, and Edmund Tilney served from 1599 to 1609 or 1610—a situation where the longer liver takes all.

Edmund Spenser fared better with the queen than most writers, but he never had his heart's desire. In 1590, when he published the first three books of the *Faerie Queene,* his main dedication was addressed to the "most magnificent Empress Elizabeth, by the grace of God, Queen of England, France, and Ireland." Some of the seventeen sonnets he added were in honor of powerful officials; the last three complimented the Countess of Pembroke, the Lady Carey, and "all the gracious and beautiful ladies of the court." Spenser did receive a gentleman's estate in Ireland with an annuity of £50 a year, but he had hoped for some high office in the government that would bring him home from exile in Ireland. That gift he never received.

Other writers dedicated many great books to the queen, with or without rewards. Perhaps they were sometimes thanked and considered that an honor worthwhile, or perhaps they hoped that a dedication to her would increase their sales to others. She was honored in 1579 by Sir Thomas North, when he published *The Lives of the Noble Grecians and Romans*. Besides being named as the chief patron of the *Faerie Queene*, in 1590, she received the dedications of the other two great heroic poems of her reign: Sir John Harington's translation of Ariosto's *Orlando Furioso*, in 1591, and the complete English version of Tasso's *Jerusalemme Liberata*, published under the title of *Godfrey of Bulloigne*, in 1600. Harington's translation was a penalty imposed upon him by the queen because he had passed about the court an unedifying narrative from Ariosto. When a copy of it came to the queen's attention, she ordered him to leave the court and not to return until he had translated the entire *Orlando Furioso*. As he was a godson and a favorite of the queen, he had every reason for dedicating his complete work to her. Other books dedicated to her included *Acts and Monuments*, or *The Book of Martyrs*, by John Foxe, 1563; Lyte's translation of the great *New Herbal or History of Plants*, by Rembert Dodoens, 1578; an outstanding work on education, *Positions*, by Richard Mulcaster, 1581; numerous books or translations on alchemy, architecture, civil and military honors, and books on many other subjects.

Of course there were reasons why the queen could not reward every man who asked her and why she did not do more for the greatest of them. She was short of funds—partly from her father's extravagance and his debasement of the coinage, partly from the flow of silver out of the New World with the resulting inflation, partly from her need to maintain a court that would be attractive to her subjects, and partly from great civil and military expenses. As she once said to the mediocre translator, Ralph Robinson, when he approached her in person, she could not reward every writer who asked her because she had to requite the fighting men for their pains—an almost impossible task, because it was hampered by the greed and graft of the officials who handled the funds for the payments. She also had to pay all the ordinary expenses of the government from her estates and from a few taxes assigned for that purpose. Parliament granted money for some extraordinary expenses, such as fortifications or extra costs of wars. But though she was fond of dramatic productions, perhaps her reluctance to reward the greatest writers also suggests that she did not place a high value on English literature.

Women as patrons of literature probably promoted imaginative and poetic work. In an age of faith, both men and women received dedications with collections of sermons and books of devotion. Because she was the ruler, Queen Elizabeth received dedications from many authors on a variety of subjects. Authors looked to men more often when they dedicated books on theories of government, on religious controversy, and other utilitarian ideas. Perhaps further documentation is needed for a firm conclusion that women encouraged imaginative and poetic works; but the idea will be supported in the discussion of three outstanding women of the period: Mary Sidney Herbert, Countess of Pembroke (1561–1621); Elizabeth Carey, Viscountess Falkland (1585–1639); and Lucy Russell, Countess of Bedford (1580?–1627). Each of these women spent her formative years in the Tudor Age: Mary Herbert had finished her contributions to literature by 1600; Elizabeth Carey was about eighteen and Lucy Russell was about twenty-three at the end of the period.

When John Davies of Hereford dedicated *The Muses' Sacrifice* in 1612, he named the three women, describing them as patrons of literature and saluting them as "the most noble and no less deservedly renowned ladies, as well darlings as patronesses of the Muses: Lucy, Countess of Bedford; Mary, Countess Dowager of Pembroke; and Elizabeth Carey (wife of Sir Henry Carey) glories of women." Since two other women in the period had borne the name Elizabeth Carey, he left no doubt about which one he meant.

Mary Sidney's services to literature were fourfold: she gave practical help and encouragement to many writers when she became the Countess of Pembroke and lived at Wilton House; she influenced the writing of her brother, Philip, during his brief life; she edited and published all his prose and his poetry after his death; she published her own translations from French and Italian and had an outstanding part in turning the Psalms into Elizabethan lyrics. Since there is no evidence that any of this work was done after 1600 (though she lived until 1621), for this discussion she belongs in the Tudor period.

Throughout her married life Wilton House was her chief home and the center of her literary influence, though she used smaller residences at Ivy Church and Ramsbury, also in Wiltshire, and one or more houses in London. After she became a dowager countess, it is interesting that she leased for herself the famous Crosby Hall in London, from 1609 to 1615, though it apparently had no connection

with her literary influence. At Wilton House she had brought together, it is said, "a noble library of books," including books of history and polity as well as the chief Italian poets. Though some of
these details were reported by John Aubrey, all of them seem highly
credible. Mary Herbert's translation from Petrarch and the concern
of Abraham Fraunce with Tasso while he was living at Wilton House
support the mention of the Italian poets. It has been said that the
library was later "dispersed," but a great fire in 1647, which destroyed all of Wilton House except the east front and nearly all the
contents of the building, may have been responsible for its loss.

The idea that Mary Herbert, with the help and consent of her
husband, made Wilton House a center of learning is supported by
much evidence. In 1599, in his dedicatory poem for *The Silkworms
and their Flies,* Thomas Moffett said that she had "never yet on
meanest scholar frowned," and he asked her influence for his study
of insects. In 1603 when Samuel Daniel wrote a dedication to William
Herbert, he said that he had learned the use and ordering of rhyme
from the worthy mother of William, and that Wilton House had
been his best school. About 1622, Walter Sweeper, writing of his
former intimate friend, Doctor Moffett (who had lived with the Herbert family some years as friend and physician) compared Wilton
House to a "little university." Thus he implied that encouragement
was extended to other men of learning, not only to poets and writers
of literary prose.

Later when John Aubrey followed the basic ideas of Daniel
and Sweeper, with the addition of specific details, he may have been
correct, at least in his general statements:

> In her time Wilton House was like a college, there were so many learn-
> ed and ingenious persons. She was the greatest patroness of wit and learning
> of any lady in her time. She was a great chemist and spent yearly a great
> deal in that study. She kept for her laborator in the house Adrian Gilbert
> . . . half-brother to Sir Walter Raleigh, who was a great chemist in those
> days. . . . She also gave an honorable yearly pension to Dr. Moffett, who
> hath writ a book *De insectis.* Also one . . . Boston, a good chemist . . . who
> did undo himself by studying the philosopher's stone, and she would have
> kept him, but he would have all the gold to himself and so died, I think, in
> a gaol.

Though other evidence is lacking for Mary Sidney Herbert's interest
in chemistry, her brother Philip studied it with John Dee; in his
more mature years he disliked astrology but continued the study of
chemistry. The countess may have encouraged it for her brother as
well as herself.

In their dedications many writers left specific comments on

the contributions Mary Sidney Herbert made to them and their literary development. Nicholas Breton, who seems to have lived at Wilton House for a time, honored her in three works, the earliest being *The Pilgrimage to Paradise Joined with the Countess of Pembroke's Love,* in 1592. Her love, as he used the term, was salvation with eternal life. In his dedicatory epistle to her he said that "your poor unworthy named poet . . . by the indiscretion of his youth, the malice of envy, and the disgrace of ingratitude had utterly perished had not the hand of your honor revived the heart of humility." And he likened her to the Duchess of Urbino. In 1597 and in 1601 Breton published other works with brief dedications to her. In *Wits Trenchmour,* 1597, he was almost certainly speaking of her when he described a lady's house as a little court, with "God daily served, religion truly preached, all quarrels avoided, peace carefully preserved, swearing not heard of, where truth was easily believed, a table fully furnished, a house richly garnished, honor kindly entertained, virtue highly esteemed, service well rewarded, and the poor blessedly relieved. . . ."

John Davies of Hereford, in addition to his praise of the three women writers mentioned earlier in this chapter, had added a number of poems at the close of his volume *Microcosmos,* in 1603. He addressed leaders of Scotland and England, included several poems to other members of the family of the Herberts, and one directed to the countess and her daughter Anne. In "Other Essays," Davies addressed two sonnets to "the right noble and well-accomplished lady, the Countess Dowager of Pembroke." In the first of them he said:

> If aught be fair or right in me, it is
> Not mine but thine, whose worth possesseth me;
> If I be all amiss, I all assign
> To shame and sorrow, sith no part is thine.

Gervase Babington, who dedicated to the countess *A Brief Conference Betwixt Man's Frailty and Faith,* in 1583, was one of several writers who lived with the family. Sent from the university to be a tutor, he apparently established himself more permanently as a friend.

Abraham Fraunce flourished about 1587 to 1633, but his poetic work was published between 1587 and 1592, when he was under the influence of Wilton House. His dedications to Mary Herbert began with *The Lamentations of Amintas for the Death of Phyllis,* 1587, continued with the *Arcadian Rhetoric,* in 1588, and *The Countess of Pembroke's Emanuel,* in 1591. He published also the first and second parts of *The Countess of Pembroke's Ivychurch,* and later a third part, adding to the title the words *Amintas Dale.* Though parts of this third section are in prose, the dedication (which is not available) is said to be a six-line Latin poem.

Samuel Daniel, who also went to Wilton House as a tutor for the older son William, perhaps about 1590, dedicated a number of works to the countess. In 1592 an edition of his sonnets, *Delia,* and a second edition with an ode and *The Complaint of Rosamond,* carried the same prose dedication to her. In part he said, "I desire only to be graced by the countenance of your protection, whom the fortune of the time hath made the happy and judicial patroness of the Muses. . . ." A later edition had also a dedicatory sonnet to the countess. In publishing his tragedy *Cleopatra* in 1594, he prefaced it with a long poem of dedication to her, beginning with the line, "Lo, here the labours which she did impose." He added that her "well-graced Antonie" had long remained alone but had wanted the company of his *Cleopatra.* (Both these tragedies, of course, followed classic techniques; and a little later, perhaps, Elizabeth Carey, Lady Falkland, followed the same theories in *The Tragedy of Miriam.*) In a fourteen-stanza poem of dedication Daniel praised Mary Sidney Herbert, among other things for her Psalms, which would be known, he said, after Wilton House had been leveled to the ground. This dedication was retained in an edition of 1623, *The Whole Works . . . in Poetry,* after her death.

Daniel dedicated to Mary Sidney Herbert some prose work also —*The First Four Books of the Civil War between the Two Houses of Lancaster and York,* closing with the statement that he had been revived by her goodness and held himself ever bound to her and her noble family, promising to do them honor and service. When he addressed *A Defense of Rhyme* to her older son William, by this time the Earl of Pembroke, he paid her the outstanding compliment referred to earlier in the chapter—that he had first been encouraged in the use of rhyme by William's "most worthy and honorable mother and received the first notion for the formal ordering of those compositions at Wilton, which I must ever acknowledge to have been my best school. . . ."

Such dedications as these indicate that an unusual relationship existed between Mary Sidney Herbert and the writers she was aiding. Often she gave the practical help of a good home as well as a personal interest; sometimes a real friendship sprang up between her or the members of her family and the writers who lived at Wilton House; occasionally joint efforts between her and a writer were planned, or she helped a poet to learn his craft, as she had encouraged Samuel Daniel. Such patronage is a different world from the one in which effusive flattery is directed to a stranger.

Many works on a variety of subjects were dedicated to the countess, with only a few others named here for illustration. The earliest, it seems, was in 1580 or 1581, when Thomas Howell addressed his *Devises* to her, praising her "virtuous life and rare wisdom," and her "honourable courtesy and sweet behavior." His ideas echoed often in future praises of her. John Taylor commemorated her in the fifth sonnet of a series with the title *The Needle's Excellency*. Many religious works, of course, were among those dedicated to her; but variety was contributed by Thomas Morley's *Canzonets*, or short songs for three voices, 1593, and Thomas Moffet's dedicatory poem, which he published in 1599 with *The Silkworms and their Flies*. Presumably Moffet was also the man Aubrey named as the author of a book on insects; he was certainly a physician attached to the household; in 1601 when Henry Herbert, Earl of Pembroke, died, he was provided with an annuity if he continued to treat the illnesses of the widow and her son.

The Countess of Pembroke was mentioned by Edmund Spenser in connection with several poems. When he published three books of the *Faerie Queene* in 1590, he addressed to her one of the seventeen sonnets at the close. The memory of her brother, he said, commanded him to worship that goodly image in her face, but she embellished the resemblance with her own virtues. Dedicating "The Ruins of Time," in *Complaints*, to her in 1591, he said that he was bound to her "by many singular favors and great graces." In his elegiac poem, "Astrophel," written for her brother, he complimented her as Clorinda, the sister, and included what he called her doleful lay, though he probably wrote also that part of the poem himself. But he dedicated the whole poem to Sidney's widow, who had become the Countess of Essex. In *Colin Clout's Come Home Again* Spenser praised the Countess of Pembroke for her brave mind, with its "heavenly gifts and graces."

John Donne joined those who admired the literary work of the countess when he wrote a poem of unknown date, "Upon the Translation of the Psalms by Sir Philip Sidney and the Countess of Pembroke his Sister." Referring to the translators as Moses and Miriam, he gave their work high praise.

Another poet connected with Wilton House, but after the son William had become the Earl of Pembroke, was William Browne (1591–1643?). Though he is almost forgotten now, he was praised by such contemporaries as John Davies of Hereford, George Wither, John Selden, Michael Drayton, and Ben Jonson. These and others wrote poems about him. Probably their poems increased his sales or his prestige more than his dedications to them would have done. Some time after the death of Mary Herbert, if his first line is a literal statement, Browne wrote a long, uninspired elegy addressed to her memory. He is also credited by many with the finest epitaph ever written for her, the one beginning, "Underneath this sable hearse, Lies the subject of all verse." But if one judges it by its quality, the first stanza seems more likely to be the work of Ben Johnson.

Mary Sidney Herbert edited and published her brother's prose and poetry after his death and also influenced his writing while he was living. In 1580 when she persuaded him to write *Arcadia*, she may have done so to relieve his brooding about his exile from court. Even at the request of the queen he had refused to apologize to the Earl of Oxford, and he had written a letter to the queen arguing against her marriage. In dedicating the work to his sister, Sidney said: "You desired me to do it, and your desire, to my heart, is an absolute commandment. Now it is done only for you, only to you. . . . For indeed, for severer eyes it is not, being but a trifle, and that triflingly handled."

The *Arcadia* was entered for publication in 1588, about two years after Sidney's death from his wound at Zutphen. A version of the work appeared in 1590, probably sponsored by Fulke Greville, but it was unsatisfactory and incomplete, leaving the third book unfinished. Sidney had started rewriting the whole work but had not progressed beyond a place within the third book. Hence choices had to be made between the old and the new version and a complete or an incomplete narrative. In 1593 a new edition called an authorized one was published. In it the story was completed, though some minor narratives begun in Sidney's revision were left unfinished, and the intentions of the author, probably as far as the sister could determine them, were carried out. It seems clear from the "Address to the Reader," that Mary Sidney Herbert was responsible for this authorized edition. The writer of the address said that "the disfigured face" with which the work had been presented earlier had "moved that noble lady to whose honor it was consecrated, to whose protection it was committed" to correct faults and remove defects. The writer made another promise for the lady: if no accident prevented, she would do more to establish the memory of her brother. In closing, he said that the work was now more than ever the Countess of Pembroke's *Arcadia*, "done as it was, for her, as it is, by her." The address was signed by H. S., almost certainly Henry Sanford, secretary of the Earl of Pembroke. He was probably acting as an agent for the countess in publishing *Arcadia*.

Astrophel and Stella was first published in 1591, five years after Sidney's death, "from a circulating manuscript, by Thomas Newman, who later in the same year printed a second version (altered in some 350 places) based on a manuscript either supplied or approved by the Sidney family." Lord Burghley ordered the first edition confiscated, presumably at the request of the family, according to Jack Stillinger; and at this time, *family* may have meant Sidney's sister. The earlier edition was full of misprints and garbled phrases: in sonnet 31 the moon is climbing the sky with a *mean* face instead of a *wan* face, and in sonnet 39 sleep is addressed as the *bathing* place, not the *baiting* place of wits. Though there may be some question about the exact date of the second edition, whether it also was issued in 1591 or later, there is no question about its comparative value. And for this corrected edition we are again indebted to the Countess of Pembroke.

Two editions of *The Defense of Poesy* were issued in 1595; one, published by Ponsonby, was edited with special care and was described as the "first authorized edition." Again the editor undoubtedly was Sidney's sister. In 1598 a volume of Sidney's work came from the press. It contained the *Arcadia,* with the author's dedication to his sister and with the "Address to the Reader" signed by H. S. for the authorized edition of 1593; certain poems called sonnets that had not appeared in print before; *The Defense of Poesy;* the *Astrophel and Stella* sonnets in their final form; and *The Lady of the May,* a minor work that had been presented to the queen at Wanstead. All these works in their final form we owe to the sister of Sir Philip Sidney.

The literary work of Mary Herbert consisted of translations— at least her known work. The "Dialogue between Two Shepherds in Praise of Astraea," apparently written for a visit of the queen, was a mere trifle. In 1592 she published two translations in one volume, with one title page listing *A Discourse of Life and Death,* written in French by Mornay, and *Antonius,* a tragedy written in French by Garnier, and adding that both were turned into English by the countess. In 1595 the *Antonius* was published alone as *The Tragedy of Antonie.*

In the *Discourse* the countess was working with material that she had probably come to know through her brother; for Philippe du Plessis Mornay had become an intimate friend of Sir Philip Sidney, when they had met earlier on the Continent. In 1577–1578 and again in 1580 Mornay was an official representative in England, urging

Queen Elizabeth to give support to the French Protestants. When the whole family came to England on one of these trips, Sidney stood as godfather to Mornay's infant daughter. It would be strange if Mornay, while he was living in England, did not meet Sidney's sister. Though we do not know when she began the translation, a work like this might take longer than a few months and might have been planned not long after the death of her brother. Through the work she may have relived happier days of the past and also struggled to reconcile herself to the loss she had endured; for Mornay emphasized both the Stoical and the Christian acceptance of death.

At some time, perhaps within the later 1580s, Mary Herbert translated also Petrarch's "Triumph of Death" from the Italian, this time emphasizing the power of death over all people of the past as well as the present and the future, without regard to rank or fame. This work remained with the Petyt manuscripts at the Inner Temple until 1912, when Frances B. Young published it as Appendix A with *Mary Sidney: Countess of Pembroke*. Admitting that the work is occasionally obscure, Miss Young praised the use of the difficult terza rima in the English version, the "astonishingly literal" quality, the "ingenuity of phrasing," and the "adroit transpositions."

Perhaps Mary Herbert turned to the translation from Petrarch about 1586, when she lost her parents and her brother Philip and was confronted with her own helplessness against the power of death. Then a little later, perhaps, she may have begun translating the Mornay as a part of her struggle to accept death. But these ideas are conjecture, since few dates for her work are available.

In the *Antonius,* the subject was death again, but without any serious possibility of relationship to the experiences of the translator herself. But in her choice of this play the countess lent support to classical or Senecan drama, with unities of time, place, action, and tragic mood; her work was followed by other plays using the same dramatic principles—Samuel Daniel's *Cleopatra, The Tragedy of Mariam* by Lady Falkland, and others. And Philip Sidney, in *The Defense of Poesy,* mainly supported the same dramatic principles.

The real claim of Mary Sidney Herbert to poetic ability, however, rests upon her poetic recreations of the Psalms. It is generally agreed that Sir Philip Sidney was responsible for the first forty-three and that she changed the others into Elizabethan poems. His work was doubtless done before his departure for the Low Countries in 1585. Her work was under way in the late 1580s or at least well before 1593, for in the latter year Samuel Daniel praised her, saying her work on the Psalms would be known after Wilton House was level with the ground. It was completed before 1600, the estimate given by J. C. A. Rathmell, the recent editor of the Psalms.

Though the Psalms of the Sidneys were passed about in manuscript, were certainly known to John Donne, and may have come into the hands of George Herbert in time to influence his *Temple,* they did not appear in print until 1823. The modern edition with an excellent introduction by Rathmell was published in 1963.

Psalms were popular during the reign of Elizabeth. They were versified and published for use in churches because the practice of singing them was acceptable to Anglican and Puritan elements alike in congregations. By 1562 *The Whole Book of Psalms* had been published, and a hundred fifty editions followed. But these were utilitarian versions. The Psalms of the Sidneys, as Rathmell said, were literature: they had "energy, intensity, and emotional piquancy," they emphasized an allegorical significance, and they used a variety of forms, adapting the form to the emotion of a particular Psalm. They were an effort to use all the resources of the Elizabethan lyric; and both Sidneys, Rathmell concluded, tried to develop for each one "a unique combination of stanza pattern and rhyme scheme" adapted to the individual Psalm.

Neither of the Sidneys, according to Rathmell, knew Hebrew. They worked by comparing versions in the psalter of the Prayer Book with the two current English translations of the Bible (the Geneva Bible, 1560, and the Bishops' Bible, 1568); they used also the elaborate commentaries on the Psalms, those of Beza having been translated into English by Gilby and those of Calvin by Golding. Mary Sidney Herbert especially often expanded an image because the commentaries gave her the right to do so. The Vulgate was available, of course, but Rathmell did not mention it and probably they would not have considered turning to it. Though both the Sidneys must have known Latin well and Sir Philip read Greek easily, for their work on the Psalms, they needed no language but English.

In his poem upon the translation of the Psalms by the Sidneys John Donne said that the Psalms abroad were well translated but were badly handled in England; also good versions were used in private homes and less good ones in churches. He concluded:

> So though some have, some may some Psalms translate,
> We thy Sidnean Psalms shall celebrate.

Perhaps no one was better fitted than Donne, poet and clergyman, to compare other translations of the Psalms with the work of the Sidneys.

Informed and judicious critics express the view that the work of Mary Herbert on the Psalms was superior to that of her brother. In the nineteenth century A. B. Grosart had said that the Psalms she translated are "infinitely in advance of her brother's in thought, epithet, and melody." Quoting him, Rathmell added that "they demand to be considered not only in the context of Elizabethan psalmody, but as significant and attractive poems in their own right." Again he said: "The Countess has, in a devotional sense, *meditated* on the text before her, and the force of her version derives from her sense of personal involvement; she has taken into account Calvin's interpretation of the verse, and it is her capacity to appreciate the underlying meaning that vivifies her lines." Quoting from *The Poetry of Meditation* by Louis L. Martz, Rathmell agreed with his statement that the work of the Sidneys was "the attempt to bring the art of the Elizabethan lyric into the service of psalmody, and to perform this in such a way that it makes the psalm an intimate personal cry to God." He also added that the comment applies "with even greater force to the Psalms of the Countess of Pembroke."

Thus Mary Sidney Herbert, Countess of Pembroke, emerges as the possessor of the greatest poetic talent among the women of her age—or perhaps the only woman who gave genuine evidence of such a talent. To many, it seems surprising that she did not write or at least did not publish original poems or other imaginative works of her own. Others who write about her think it quite possible that she did such writing but modestly passed it about unsigned to a few friends; thus it was assigned to others or it was lost. Some evidence for the speculation comes from the fact that the Sidney Psalms were known to John Donne and other contemporaries of Mary Sidney, but they did not appear in print before 1823. But her admirers left a wealth of comment on her, and if she had been known to any of them as the author of original poems, they would surely have revealed that knowledge. As a patron of literature, however, no woman excelled her in practical help; no other gave writers a home, with food, lodging, instruction in writing, and the intellectual stimulus of a university.

Elizabeth Carey, mentioned earlier in the dedication to her with Mary Sidney and Lucy Russell, was the daughter of Sir Lawrence Tanfield; she married Henry Carey when she was about fifteen. In 1620 her husband became Viscount Falkland; but perhaps she did

not use the term Viscountess Falkland or Lady Falkland herself because they separated when he discovered that she had secretly become
a Catholic. She was said to have mastered Latin early and later to
have taught herself French, Spanish, Italian, and Hebrew. Her biographers, chiefly a son and a daughter, did not mention Greek. Her
reading included all the poetry she could find in several different languages, many French writers, Greek and Roman history, all the chronicles of England, and much church history—St. Jerome, St. Gregory,
St. Augustine, other early fathers of the church, and the whole controversy, including Luther, Calvin, Latimer, and Bishop Jewel. After
the reading of the early fathers changed her into a Catholic, she was
especially devoted to the writings of Sir Thomas More, presumably
his religious writings.

She wrote, it seems, almost as much as she read. Before her
marriage she had translated the epistles of Seneca. She translated
Cardinal Perron's reply to the attack of King James on his work, but
by an official order it was burned. Then she translated the whole
body of Perron's work into English for the use of scholars at Oxford
and Cambridge, but it was never published. She wrote in verse lives
of St. Mary Magdalene, St. Agnes the Martyr, and St. Elizabeth of
Portugal, and many hymns in honor of the Virgin Mary. But they
also remained in manuscript. Hence one cannot estimate her skill
but only her industry.

Lady Falkland wrote also two plays. One of them *The Tragedy
of Mariam,* with its source in Josephus and its setting in Palestine, was
published and thus survived. In the past it was assumed to be the
work of the Elizabeth Carey who was the daughter of George Carey,
second Baron Hundson. But in 1914, A. C. Dunstan, who edited the
play for the Malone Society, established the fact that the play was
written by the Elizabeth Carey who was Lady Falkland. Besides in-
ternal evidence (which it seems unnecessary to repeat here), he found
two pieces of external evidence. One of these was a dedicatory sonnet,
in the Huth Library copy of the play, addressed to Elizabeth Bland
Carey, the wife of Sir Henry Carey's brother Philip. The other was
part of the dedication, mentioned earlier in the chapter, that John
Davies of Hereford offered, with *The Muses' Sacrifice,* in 1612, to the
three outstanding women discussed in this chapter. There he not only
identified her as the wife of Sir Henry Carey but also as the play-
wright, when he said:

> Thou makest Melpomen proud, and my heart great
>   of such a pupil, who in buskin fine
> With feet of state, dost make thy muse to greet
>   the scenes of Syracuse and Palestine.

The scenes of Syracuse apparently refer to another play, but it is not extant and was probably never published. When Davies spoke of Lady Falkland as his pupil he probably referred to his teaching of calligraphy.

Dunstan described *The Tragedy of Mariam* as one of the most regular of all classic dramas, with its nuntius, lack of action, division into five acts, small number of characters, use of a chorus and of much exposition, and its absence of comic scenes. Thus it follows the tradition favored by Sir Philip Sidney in his *Defense of Poesy* and by his sister Mary when she translated her *Antonie* and influenced Samuel Daniel to write his *Cleopatra*. *The Tragedy of Mariam* was also the first drama and perhaps the only drama known to have been written and published within the English Renaissance by a woman.

Elizabeth Carey, Lady Falkland, received other dedications—though it seems impossible to determine the extent to which she encouraged writers with gifts. Possibly she merely stirred their admiration. An early dedication by Michael Drayton appeared in *England's Heroical Epistles,* preceding the epistle of William de la Pole, Duke of Suffolk, to Queen Margaret. Drayton published the work in 1599, addressing the lady in conventional and effusive terms as Elizabeth Tanfield.

In 1614 the second edition of *England's Helicon* had a dedicatory sonnet signed by the printer, Richard More, and addressed to "the truly virtuous and honorable lady, the Lady Elizabeth Carey." In 1614 only one woman bore that name, for the widow of Baron Hundson had married Lord Eure, and her daughter by that name had married Thomas Berkeley about 1595 or 1596.

In 1633 the *Works* of John Marston had a dedicatory sonnet addressed "to the right honorable, the Lady Elizabeth Carey, Viscountess Falkland." Signed by William Sheares in the author's absence, it was effusive: "your Honour is well acquainted with the Muses. . . . Fame hath given out that your Honour is the mirror of your sex, the admiration not only of this island but of all adjacent countries and dominions which are acquainted with your rare virtues and endowments. . . ." It seems that her contemporaries honored Lady Falkland more than we might expect, and later centuries, perhaps a little less than she deserves.

Lucy Harington Russell, Countess of Bedford, was a friend to poets and a glamorous inspiration to them. She was the daughter of that John Harington who became Baron Harington at the accession

of James in 1603 and whose wife was Anne Kelway. Her father was
a cousin of Sir John Harington, the irrepressible godson of the queen.
In 1594, when Lucy was thirteen or fourteen, she was married to the
nineteen-year-old Edward Russell, third Earl of Bedford.

Little is known about her education, but members of the families with which she was connected valued education, received dedications of books, collected libraries, and were known as patrons of
literature. She had unusual artistic taste (Sir William Temple praised
the garden she developed at Moor Park, Hertfordshire, her home after
1617, as the most beautiful one he had seen in England or in any
other country), her reputation as a collector of coins and medals suggests training in the classics, and she certainly had literary tastes and
interests. But she did nothing to prove that she was a scholar in
either Greek or Latin. Perhaps she was educated by tutors, along
with her brother John, who was praised for his early mastery of Greek,
Italian, French, and Latin.

It seems certain that the Countess of Bedford wrote poems
herself. About 1606 John Donne suggested that she had let him see
some of them when they were together in Twickenham Garden, her
earlier home after her marriage. Wishing to see them again, he wrote,
"I humbly beg them of your ladyship, with two promises . . . that I
will not show them, and that I will not believe them. . . ." But she
published no work under her name, and so far nobody seems to have
found manuscripts of her poems. Thus we have no way of estimating
her creative ability, and her importance rests solely upon the encouragement she gave to others. It is possible that she wrote the well-
known poem beginning. "Death, be not proud, thy hand gave not
this blow." Editors usually place it among the poems attributed to
Donne, but two manuscript versions, it is said, indicate that it was
written by the countess herself. In discussing the poem, R. C. Bald
leaves the question of authorship without a final answer—as this
writer also must do. But whoever wrote the poem had creative ability.

Of course she is remembered chiefly as a patron of poets. She
did extravagant entertaining of literary men, presumably gave them
many gifts, had many poems written to her or about her, and received
many other dedications. Of those listed in *The Index of Dedications*,
about a half dozen were addressed to her and her husband; some to
her and other people or other women, such as the dedication of *The
Muses' Sacrifice* by John Davies of Hereford to the three women emphasized in this chapter; and others to her alone. In his "Sonnets to
Worthy Persons," Davies included one for her. In the dedications
with his translation of Homer, George Chapman addressed to her one
sonnet of the dozen he placed at the close of his work.

Michael Drayton honored her many times. Some have suggested that his relationship to her cooled, but Oliver Elton, in his critical study of Drayton, has refuted the idea with apparent success. Early in 1594 Drayton dedicated *Matilda* to her while she was still Lucy Harington. In 1595 he recognized her new status as a countess by publishing his "Great Lady" sonnet as a preface to *Endimion and Phoebe*. He used the same sonnet, Elton stated, with some version of *Idea*, four times from 1599 through 1605. In 1597 he dedicated *England's Heroical Epistles* as a whole to her, with separate epistles to her husband, to her mother, and to Mistress Tanfield. This dedication to her appeared again in 1598, 1599, 1602, and perhaps in later editions.

Drayton dedicated to Lucy Russell his *Mortimeriados* in 1596, with nine stanzas in her honor. When he published an entirely different version of the material in 1603 as the *Barons' Wars*, it is true that he dedicated it to Sir Walter Aston. But Aston was also a long-time friend and patron; furthermore, he was one of the richest men in England, with the rental value of his inherited lands estimated at £10,000 a year. When an author published the same book again or issued a new version of it, he often chose another person for his dedication, with no apparent reason except to honor another friend. Drayton reprinted his "Great Lady" sonnet with the *Barons' Wars*, along with a number of other sonnets, and followed it with one to the mother of the countess, Lady Anne Harington. If all these details are correct (and the many editions are not available for checking), Drayton's attitude to Lucy, Countess of Bedford, did not change. Probably he received from her many gifts.

Samuel Daniel did not fail to include Lucy Russell in his dedications; when he published *Certain Epistles,* in 1601–1603 (to repeat details mentioned earlier), he dedicated one epistle to her. His masque, "The Vision of the Twelve Goddesses," presented earlier at Hampton Court and published about the same time, was issued again in 1623 with a long, explanatory dedication to her.

In 1624 *The Works of that Late . . . and Learned Divine, Mr. T. Wilcox,* were dedicated to the Earl of Bedford and his "right Honourable Lady." The treatises included in the volume had been published separately, with dedications to various people. But when the printer offered John Burgess the opportunity to dedicate the collected works, he accepted willingly because he had married a daughter of Wilcox, he had always valued these works, and he welcomed a chance to honor the Earl and the Countess of Bedford. To them he owed "more than to all the world beside," for their "princelike, great, and immerited favors unto me, even unto me, poor man, who can make no manner of answerable return." Unless words deceive, this dedication was sincere.

But the greatest contribution of Lucy Russell to literature was her influence on individual poems by Ben Jonson and John Donne. Jonson referred to her or addressed her directly in a number, including some of his best poems. Using as a title for one, "In the Form of a Grace," he asked God to bless king and queen and "Bedford keep safe." His ode beginning "Splendor! O more than mortal," was written to her, the evidence being in a Rawlinson manuscript at the Bodleian, it is said, with the notation, "To Lucy, C. of B." In the poem Jonson praised her not only for splendor and brightness, but for her wit, as quick and lively as fire, and for her judgment and her learning.

Three of Jonson's epigrams were written about the countess or for her. The first of these, "On Lucy, Countess of Bedford," is serious as well as complimentary. The author began by asking himself what kind of person he would like to honor with his poems. He answered that he would choose one who is fair, free, wise, great in blood but more good than great, courteous, sweet, free from pride, and one who manages daily life well. His Muse told him that he need not invent, but only write, "Lucy, Countess of Bedford." Another epigram is only a light, humorous form of begging. Though he had asked a lord for a buck, the lord refused him; when Lucy offered him one, probably killed in her park, he had not answered. Now he wishes her to send him one, and he describes the inspiration that would be his as a result.

For the third epigram Jonson used the title, "Lucy, Countess of Bedford, with Master Donne's Satires," sending it to her presumably with a manuscript copy of the poems. The poem, one of Jonson's best-known and perhaps one of his best, begins:

> Lucy, you brightness of our sphere, who are
> Life of the Muses' day, their morning star!

Lucy Russell also influenced the masques of Ben Jonson, after she began appearing at the court. Under Elizabeth she had no position there, probably because her husband preferred his home and his library. He was so detached from political affairs that he became quite innocently involved in the Essex rebellion when Penelope Rich came in her carriage, saying that her brother wished to see him at Essex House. Later when James I offered to make him a Knight of the Bath, he managed to evade the honor.

Lucy Russell's quiet days ended for a time in 1603 with the

accession of the king. She and her mother joined "a flight of ladies" who hurried north to greet the new queen and offer their services to her. At the time, the Earl of Bedford may still have been in prison because of his alleged involvement in the Essex affair. Queen Anne cordially received the ladies, immediately appointed Lucy to the privy chamber, soon named Lucy's parents as caretakers for her daughter Elizabeth, and bestowed on Lucy's father the title, Baron Harington of Exton. Lucy, who was only twenty-three years old when James came to the throne, assumed a prominent place in court. According to R. C. Bald, she became the closest friend of the queen, and from 1603 to about 1620 she was "one of the most influential women in England."

In her new status, she encouraged Ben Jonson in his writing of court masques, according to J. H. Wiffen, and she also promoted their production at the court. She, the queen herself, and ten other ladies of the court took the chief parts in the "Masque of Blackness," presented at Whitehall, for Twelfth Night, 1605, at a cost of £3,000. When Jonson prepared his "Masque of Hymen," for the marriage of young Robert, Earl of Essex, to Frances Howard, in January, 1606, Lucy was one of the eight nuptial powers of Juno Pronuba. She appeared in the "Masque of Beauty" in 1608, and in Jonson's "Masque of Queens," preceded by his "Antemasque of Witches," February 2, 1609. Though the queen continued to display her physical charms in these extravaganzas, Lucy did not take part in any future masque. Since she kept up other connections with the court, the reason is not apparent.

Probably Lucy Russell influenced John Donne even more than she influenced Ben Jonson. Though it may be difficult to say when the friendship began, they were meeting often by the summer of 1607 and were corresponding, many of their exchanges being in verse. In August, 1608, she was godmother to Donne's daughter Lucy, and undoubtedly attended the festivities connected with the baptism of the child. The friendship, said R. C. Bald, grew with "rapidity and fervour." He added: "There was a strong element of mutual attraction. . . . She possessed, besides rank and wealth, youth and charm as well as wit and an unusual share of intellectual capacity, and all these qualities attracted Donne to her. She . . . found something intoxicating in the brilliance of his mind and in the quality of his flattery."

In 1609 Donne acted almost as if he were "Lady Bedford's officially appointed laureate." When her cousin Bridget, Lady Markham, died in May of that year, and her intimate friend, Cecilia Bulstrode, died some weeks later, he wrote an elegy for each—poems that are artificial and lack warmth of feeling. In 1614 when John Harington, the brother of the countess, died, Donne composed for him a long elegy that pleased her. Beginning with a short epistle addressed to her, he developed the poem, "Obsequies to the Lord Harington, Brother to the Lady Lucy, Countess of Bedford." Though he had known the young man several years and, it is said, liked him, he probably did not feel keen personal sorrow. As a result, he tended to exaggerate statements, like his concluding resolve to bury his muse in the grave of this young man as Alexander had ordered whole towns destroyed because of his loss. He sent the poem to the countess with a letter begging for some recompense.

In her first enthusiasm about the elegy Donne had written for her brother, the countess told Donne that she would pay off his debts. Later she found that to be impossible. She gave him thirty pounds, explained her own financial troubles, and said that she hoped to do more in future. Whether she was able to do so at any future time seems unlikely. A letter Donne wrote to his friend, Sir Henry Goodyer (asking him to burn it after he had read it) made clear his bitter disappointment. Donne did have serious problems at the time—an imprudent marriage, a large family, his own illness, trouble with his eyes that might have caused blindness, and a large debt, with creditors demanding payment. He was planning to enter the church, and he had hoped first to settle all his finances. He and Lucy remained friends, but the frequent meetings, begun about 1607, ended about 1615. In the latter year he was ordained deacon and priest at St. Paul's Cathedral, and his new duties reduced his chances of seeing her.

The character of Lucy Russell, both as a human being and a patron of literature, cannot be estimated without knowledge of the many reasons why she could not pay Donne's debts. The situation has often been dismissed with a mention of extravagance—in buying a collection of Holbeins without considering the cost, in earlier gifts to literary men, and in lavish entertaining at Twickenham.

But other causes, mostly outside her control, have not been sufficiently stressed. Her father had been ruined financially because he and Lady Harington were made responsible for the care and education of the Princess Elizabeth. The annual pension allowed them by King James (£1,500 at first and later £2,500) was inadequate; for the princess had expensive tastes and was determined to indulge them. In 1613 they had "to buy her bridal trousseau and arrange the expenses of her wedding." For one year only, 1612–1613, her current expenses left Baron Harington with a debt of £3,500. At his death in

1613, his widow was left in poverty. When Lucy's brother succeeded to the title and the estate, he felt obliged to sell the family seat, Exton House. He died of smallpox in 1614, leaving one-third of his estate to his other sister, Lady Chichester, and two-thirds to Lucy Russell.

Lucy Russell had other family obligations also. After the death of Lady Chichester in 1615, she felt obliged to arrange a marriage portion for the daughter of that sister, especially since she had promoted the marriage. For that settlement she gave up most of the property she had from the will of her brother. At the same time she was involved in another family problem: Sir John Harington had brought suit against her mother, but the outcome of the suit would have a direct effect on her.

And she had other problems of accident and illness. In 1612 her husband had been thrown from his horse; he remained partly paralyzed. In 1612–1613 she had a serious illness from which she barely recovered in time to take part in the wedding of the Princess Elizabeth.

Her finances apparently forced her to abandon a project she had begun, that of erecting a family monument to the Haringtons. The records of Nicholas Stone, as reported by W. L. Spiers, make clear that she had commissioned him in 1616 to erect such a monument, at a cost of more than a thousand pounds. After her death in 1627, Stone sold the Earl of Middlesex a skeleton made for it, with a promise to return it if it were ever needed for the Harington tomb. When she promised Donne to pay off his debts and when she gave the commission for the tomb, probably she had not yet realized fully the failure of the family fortunes.

But John Donne's poems inspired by Lucy, Countess of Bedford, remain. They have been often discussed, and nothing new can be added here. Besides composing for her the elegies mentioned above, he wrote at least six poems with a main title "To the Countess of Bedford," and another, "To the Lady Bedford," doubtless intended for her. An "Epitaph on Himself" carried a subtitle, "To the Countess of Bedford." Another with her name used as the main title added a subheading, "Begun in France but never perfected." His aim in it was to convince her that he did not value other patrons above her. Donne did have other patrons, both men and women; they included Sir Robert Drury, whose daughter's death led him to write the *Anniversary* poems, a Mistress Cokayne (mother of a minor poet, Sir Aston Cokayne), Lady Magdalen Herbert (mother of the poet, George Herbert), the Countess of Huntingdon (Elizabeth Stanley, daughter of Alice Spencer), and the Countess of Salisbury.

Perhaps one might nominate as Donne's best poem addressed to Lucy Russell the one beginning with these lines:

> Reason is our soul's left hand, faith her right,
> By these we reach divinity, that's you:
> Their loves, who have the blessings of your light
> Grew from their reason, mine from fair faith grew.

Perhaps also it can be said that John Donne's poems addressed to Lucy Russell, Countess of Bedford, when considered as courtly compliment, are unexcelled.

King James gave no encouragement whatever to the literary pursuits of women like Elizabeth Carey, Mary Sidney Herbert, and Lucy Russell. His court, compared with those presided over by Catherine of Aragon, Catherine Parr, and Queen Elizabeth, had no intellectual life for women. "Unfortunately the death of Elizabeth marked the end of a favorable attitude to women," said G. D. Meyer as he surveyed the transition to the seventeenth century. He added, "James I had no intention of lending his support to a movement he did not countenance." His queen was frivolous, without any intellectual interests. His own fondness for handsome young men needs no documentation.

According to the French ambassador, Beaumont, the king took pride in showing his contempt for women: "They are obliged to kneel before him when they are presented, he exhorts them openly to virtue, and scoffs with great levity at men who pay them honor." His prurient curiosity about the details of the bridal night when his favorites married and when his own daughter was a bride did nothing to endear him to ladies of the court. Neither did the frequent filth of his dress and his person, nor the scandalous and drunken behavior at the court, as it was reported by Lady Anne Clifford in her *Diary*, in 1603, and by Sir John Harington, writing in 1606 to Mr. Secretary Barlow.

The education of King James in Scotland had not emphasized either the right or the ability of women to pursue a sound classical education. And in a frivolous, extravagant, drunken court, he could hardly be expected to encourage them. The few highly learned women in the seventeenth century probably developed in spite of King James.

Perhaps Mary Astell had reason in *A Serious Proposal to the Ladies,* about 1694, when she said to women: "We will therefore inquire what it is that stops your flight, that keeps you groveling here below, like Domitian catching flies, when you should be busy in obtaining empires." She urged the women of her day to spend less time in decorating their bodies and more in developing their minds and to stop being "little useless and impertinent animals." She quoted William Wotton, whose *Reflections on Ancient and Modern Learning* had just been published and who had said of the sixteenth century:

It [learning] was so very modish that the fair sex seemed to believe that Greek and Latin added to their charms, and Plato and Aristotle untranslated were frequent ornaments of their closets. One would think by the effects that it was a proper way of educating them, since there are no accounts in history of so many great women in any one age as are to be found between the years 1500 and 1600.

A P P E N D I X

OTHER NOTEWORTHY WOMEN

ASCHAM, MARGARET HOWE (1535?–1590 or 1592). Came of "a good, though not wealthy, county family from South Ockenden in Essex," said L. V. Ryan. At marriage to Ascham, then about twice her age, was a young, attractive girl with another ardent suitor. Was a loyal wife. Published her husband's important work, *The Scholemaster,* in 1570, after his death in December, 1568. Wrote with good taste and judgment a dedication addressed to Sir William Cecil, asking him "to auaunce the good that may come of it by your allowance . . . to public use and benefite. . . ." —*DNB.* Ascham, *The Scholemaster,* 1570. L. V. Ryan, *Roger Ascham,* Stanford, London, 1963.

DORMER, JANE (1538–1612). Daughter of Wm. Dormer and his wife, a Mary Sidney. Niece of Sebastian Newdigate, a Carthusian monk executed in 1535. Favorite attendant of Queen Mary, who at death, asked her to deliver jewels and messages to Princess Elizabeth. In December, 1558, married Count of Feria and went to live in Estramadura, Spain. There she supported and founded religious houses, did beautiful needlework, read devout books, gave generously to the poor and to gentlemen in misfortune, including non-Catholic Englishmen like Richard Hawkins, imprisoned in Madrid. An excellent manager. Appointed by the count at his death, with praise of her ability, to care for the estate and guide the eleven-year-old son and heir. Cleared a huge debt before her son took over at twenty-five. Perhaps hoped to become governor of Flanders in 1592. —*DNB.* Beatrice White, *Mary Tudor,* New York, 1935. Henry Clifford, *The Life of Jane Dormer, Duchess of Feria,* ed. Jos. Stevenson, London, 1887.

GREY, ELIZABETH, DUCHESS OF KENT (1581–1651). Daughter of Gilbert Talbot, Earl of Shrewsbury, and Mary Cavendish, his wife. Granddaughter of Bess of Hardwick. Before September, 1623, married Henry Grey, Earl of Kent, who died without issue in 1639. Was perhaps mentioned in *Table Talk* by John Selden, eminent jurist, legal adviser, and intimate friend of Henry Grey. Author of a work in two parts, with separate title pages but continuous paging: 1. *A Choice Manual, or Rare and Select Secrets in Physic and Chirurgery,* and 2. *A True Gentlewoman's Delight . . . All Manner of Cookery.* A first edition without date, a second in 1653, with many editions following. —*DNB. Complete Peerage,* London, 1910–1959. Donald Wing, *STC . . . 1641–1700.*

GRIMSTON, ELIZABETH (1563?–1603). Daughter of Martin Bernye, of Gunton, Norfolk. Wife of Christopher Grimston of Grimston, Yorkshire, by 1584. Her mature life made miserable by her mother's virulent hate (perhaps from religious differences), so that she became a chronic invalid and "a dead woman among the living." Decided to "break the barren soil of her fruitless brain"; began a moral guidebook for her son Bernye. Result: *Miscellanea, Meditations, Memoratives,* first published in 1604, after her death, with three other editions by 1610. Admired and quoted poems by Catholic writers, including those by her kinsman, Robert Southwell. —*DNB. STC* 12407–12411. Ruth Hughey and Philip Hereford, "Elizabeth Grymeston and her *Miscellanea,*" *Library,* XV (1934–1935), 61–91.

PARRY, BLANCHE (1508–1590). Daughter of Henry Parry, New Court, Hereford. Chief gentlewoman of Elizabeth's privy chamber for many years. An encourager of learning, according to George Ballard. Persuaded queen to give John Dee the mastership of St. Cross when his fortunes were uncertain. Godmother for Dee's son Arthur in 1579, but Dee recorded that Mistress Aubrey was a deputy for "my cousin, Mistress Blanche Parry." Communicated "to that great antiquary, Dr. Powell, Sir Edward Stradling's manuscript history of *The Winning of Glamorgan,*" according to one account. —George Ballard, *Memoirs of British Ladies,* London, 1775. John Dee, *Diary,* ed. J. O. Halliwell, Camden Society, 19 (1842).

SIDNEY, FRANCES (1584–1612). Daughter of Sir Philip Sidney. Queen as her godmother. Married Roger Manners, Earl of Rutland, but died without issue. Received high praise from Ben Johnson in his "Conversations": she was "nothing inferior to her father in poesie." —*Complete Peerage,* London, 1910–1959.

TISHEM, CATHERINE (fl. 1560–1570). English by birth. Married Walter Gruter, citizen and merchant of Antwerp. Settled in Norwich with her husband after he had signed a strong protest against the tyranny of Philip II. Mother of a son, Jean, or Janus. Catherine knew well French, Latin, and Italian, it is said, and was proficient in Greek, reading Galen with ease in the original. The son entered Caius College, later studied at Leyden, held a professorship at Heidelberg, including the direction of the library. Was able, as a result, to publish commentaries on most authors of ancient Rome. Became an eminent philologist. Basis of her reputation, her success in giving her son his early education. —George Ballard, *Memoirs of British Ladies,* London, 1775. Pierre Bayle, *A General Dictionary,* London, 1737 (under *Gruter*).

TYLER, MARGARET (fl. 1578–1601). Published in 1578 a translation from the Spanish of Diego Ortuñez de Calahorra, as *The Mirror of Princely Deeds.* Unknown except for this work and details given in it. Dedicated to Thomas, Lord Howard, because of the special benefits she had received from his parents while they lived, she "then being their servant." In an address to the reader, mentioned her delight in the Spanish, apologized for the masculine subject matter but then defended it, saying that men had dedicated to women books on law, physic, government, and war, and a woman might translate whatever a woman might read. Other writers followed her lead with translations from Ortuñez. —*STC* under *Tyler*, after 24414; also 18859–18871.

WESTON, ELIZABETH JANE (1582–1612). Born in London but taken to Prague with her family by her father, either a political rebel or a zealous Catholic. Lived in or near Prague several years. In 1597, the family left almost destitute by the sudden death of her father. Gradually won interest of influential people through her personality and the quality of her Latin poems, with the vice-chancellor of Bohemia, Heinrich von Pisnitz, and the learned Canon Georg Barthold Pontanus von Braitenberg coming to her aid. Her poems (chiefly addresses to princes, epigrams, translations, or epistles to friends) collected and publication paid for by a Silesian nobleman, Georg Martin von Baldhoven, in 1602. Married Johann Leon, an agent at the Imperial Court for the Duke of Brunswick and the Prince of Anhalt, about 1602. High praise of her Latin poems from Scaliger, Justus Lipsius, and others, and from English scholars also. Spoke chiefly German, but always wrote, prose or verse, in Latin. A skilled calligrapher and an accomplished linguist, it is said, "speaking and writing perfectly the English, German, Greek, Latin, Italian and Czech languages." —*DNB*.

WITHYPOLL, ELIZABETH (1510–1537). Daughter of Paul Withypoll, of London, and sister of Edmund Withypoll, a favorite student of Thomas Lupset. Married Emmanuel Lucar, an important member of the Merchant Taylors Company and one of three members influential in founding their school. Had a tablet of brass erected by her husband in the London church where she was buried, at age 27, proclaiming her accomplishments: her intricate needlework; her beautiful writing in "three manner hands"; her singing in "diverse languages"; her performance on the viol, lute, and virginal; her writing, reading, and speaking "with perfect utterance" Italian, Spanish, and Latin; her excellent use of English; her virtues; and her religious faith. An outstanding example of a middle-class woman educated in the classics. —George Ballard, *Memoirs of British Ladies*, London, 1775. Chas. M. Glode, *The Early History of the Guild of Merchant Taylors*, London, 1888. John A. Gee, *The Life and Works of Thomas Lupset*, London, 1928.

WROTH, LADY MARY (1586?–1640). Oldest daughter of Robert Sidney (younger brother of Sir Philip and the first Earl of Leicester of the second creation). Married Sir Robert Wroth, of Loughton Hall, Essex, but at his death in 1614, was childless. From about 1605, a recognized patroness of literature. Received from Ben Jonson the dedication of *The Alchemist* in 1610, and also a sonnet and two epigrams in *Underwoods* were addressed to her. In 1621 published *The Countess of Montgomery's Urania*, naming it to compliment her friend and neighbor, Susan, first wife of Philip Herbert (the younger son of Mary, Countess of Pembroke), who became Earl of Montgomery in 1605. Susan: the daughter of Earl of Oxford and Anne Cecil, and the granddaughter of Lord Burghley. *Urania*, an inferior imitation of her uncle's *Arcadia*, a story of princes and princesses in the guise of shepherds and shepherdesses. Has been called "tedious, long-winded, awkward," but also satiric, with courtiers able to recognize themselves in some characters. Published also a separate collection of poems, with 20 songs and 100 sonnets, many of them having genuine poetic quality. —*DNB. STC* 26051.

Other women mentioned for education in the classics, translations, or some publication of prose or verse: Margaret Blauer (fl. 1525 in Constance). Elizabeth Melville Colville (fl. 1603). Jane Meautys Cornwallis (1581–1659). Eleanor Davies (1590–1652). Angell Day (fl. 1586). Anne Dowriche (fl. 1589). Lady Elizabeth Fane (fl. 1550). Mary MacLeod (1569–1674). Pirckheimer sisters (fl. 1524 in Nuremberg). Diana Primrose (fl. 1600). Lady Anne Southwell (1573?–1636). Agnes Wenman (? –1617).

Other women mentioned for the ownership of books: Alice Edwards owned 12 books in 1546, by an inventory on her decease; Judith Isham of Lamport Hall, Northamptonshire, about 1636, listed 16 under the label, "A note of my mother's books in the chest"; a woman named Walter, about 1615, gave 56 books to Ipswich Old Town Library. —Sears Jayne, *Library Catalogues of the English Renaissance*, Berkeley, 1956.

HISTORICAL BACKGROUND

BEAUFORTS (descendants of John of Gaunt, son of Edw. III and his mistress, Catherine Swynford, later his third wife)

JOHN OF GAUNT	1340–1399
JOHN BEAUFORT, Earl of Somerset (son of John of Gaunt)	1373?–1410
JOHN BEAUFORT, Duke of Somerset (grandson of John of Gaunt)	1403–1444
MARGARET BEAUFORT (dau. and heir of Duke of Somerset; first husband, Edmund Tudor, son of Owen Tudor and Catherine of France, widow of Henry V)	1443–1509

STUART RULERS, SCOTLAND

JAMES IV (m. Margaret Tudor, dau. of Henry VIII of England)	1488–1513
Regency	1513–1524

JAMES V (son of Jas. IV and Margaret T.; m. Mary
    of Guise)   1524–1542
    Regency   1542–1561
MARY QUEEN OF SCOTS   1561–1567
    Regency   1567–1578
JAMES VI (son of Mary Queen of Scots and Lord
    Darnley)   1578?–1625

SOME PRE-TUDOR RULERS, ENGLAND

EDWARD I   1272–1307
EDWARD II   1307–1327
EDWARD III (seven sons, oldest died before father, two
    others died young)   1327–1377
RICHARD II (second son of Edw. III)   1377–1399
HENRY IV (son of John of Gaunt by first wife,
    Blanche of Lancaster)   1399–1413
HENRY V (son of Henry IV)   1413–1422
HENRY VI (son of Henry V and Catherine of France).
    Two periods of rule   1429–1461
                                                            1470–1471
EDWARD IV (descendant of Edw. III by younger son,
    Duke of York)   1461–1470
                                                            1471–1483
EDWARD V (older son of Edw. IV, nominal king April
    9–June 26, 1483, but murdered in the Tower)
RICHARD III (brother of Edw. IV)   1483–1485

TUDOR RULERS, ENGLAND (Henry VII, his son, and his three grandchildren)

HENRY VII (son of Edmund Tudor and Margaret
    Beaufort)   1485–1509
HENRY VIII (son of Henry VII and Elizabeth of York,
    dau. of Edw. IV)   1509–1547
EDWARD VI (son of Henry VIII by 3rd wife, Jane Sey-
    mour)   1547–1553
MARY TUDOR (dau. of Henry VIII by first wife, Cath-
    erine of Aragon)   1553–1558

ELIZABETH TUDOR (dau. of Henry VIII by second wife,
Anne Boleyn)   1558–1603

STUART RULERS, ENGLAND

JAMES I (also Jas. VI of Scotland, descendant of Mar-
garet Tudor)   1603–1625
CHARLES I (son of Jas. I and Anne of Denmark)   1625–1649
    Protectorate. Oliver and Richard Cromwell   1649–1660
CHARLES II (son of Chas. I and Henrietta Maria)   1660–1685
JAMES II (son of Chas. I and Henrietta Maria and
bro. of Chas. II)   1685–1688

The Tudor line ended in 1603 with the death of Queen Elizabeth, since no son or daughter of Henry VIII had any child. The
right of Henry VII to the throne came from his mother, Margaret
Beaufort. The right of James I to the English throne came from his
ancestor, Margaret Tudor. If the Suffolk line had ever reached the
throne, it also would have done so through female inheritance, by
Mary Tudor, the younger daughter of Henry VII, who married
Charles Brandon, Duke of Suffolk. Their only son died in 1533 as an
adolescent. Their older daughter, Frances, married Henry Grey; the
Greys had no surviving son; the oldest of their three daughters was
Lady Jane Grey. But though Henry VIII apparently favored the
Suffolk line and Edward VI definitely did so (perhaps because of their
English birth and background) Queen Elizabeth did not.

NOTES AND SOURCES

CHAPTER ONE: Advice to Be Passive and Subservient

Aylmer, John. *An Harborowe for Faithfull and Trewe Subjects agaynst the Late Blowne Blaste concerning the Government of Wemen.* 1559. *STC* 1005.

Barker [Bercher], Wm. *The Nobility of Women,* ed. R. Warwick Bond. London, 1904. The name often appears as Bercher. Some important comments, 151–154.

Bruts, G. M. [Bruto, Giovanni Michele]. *The Necessarie, Fit, and Convenient Education of a Yong Gentlewoman,* trans. W. P. 1598. *STC* 3947, 7499.

Camden, Carroll. *The Elizabethan Woman.* Houston, New York, London, 1952. General background.

E., T. *The Lawes Resolutions of Womens Rights.* 1632. Eve's act as the reason for woman's subjection, Bk. I, sec. iii. *STC* 7437.

Fenton, Geoffrey. *A Forme of Christian Pollicie.* 1574. *STC* 10793ᵃ.

"How the Goode Wif Thaught hir Daughter," ed. Charles Hindley for *The Old Book Collector's Miscellany.* London, 1872. For this version with many details, see II, 2–17. Or see EETS, ex. ser., XXIX (1877, rpt. 1957).

Jerome, St. *Select Letters,* trans. F. A. Wright. London, New York, 1933. See "A Girl's Education," Letter CVII; also Letter CXXVIII.

Kelso, Ruth. *Doctrine for a Lady of the Renaissance.* Urbana, 1956. Qualities of the lady and the gentleman, 23–25.

Knox, John. *The First Blast of the Trumpet against the Monstruous Regiment of Women.* Geneva, 1558. *STC* 15070. For efforts of Knox to mollify Elizabeth, see Arber (ed.), London, 1878, Appendix, 57–62.

La Tour Landry, Geoffrey de. *Here Begynneth the Book Whiche the Knyght of the Toure Made.* 1484. *STC* 15296.

Mulcaster, Richard. *Positions.* 1581. Ability of women to speak classical languages, 168. *STC* 18253.

Nichols, F. M. (ed.) *The Epistles of Erasmus.* London, New York, Bombay, 1901. Freedom to kiss English women, I, No. 98.

Rogers, Elizabeth F. *Saint Thomas More: Selected Letters.* New Haven, London, 1961. Quotation from letter to Gonell, 105.

Rye, W. B. *England as Seen by Foreigners.* London, 1865. Observations of Duke Frederick, 7–14; of Van Meteren, 69–73; of Kiechel, 89–90.

Sandys, Edwin. *The Sermons,* ed. John Eyre. Cambridge, 1841. Parker Society, vol. 41. "The Sixteenth Sermon," 313–330.

Smith, Henry. *A Preparative to Marriage.* 1591. The wife's obedience, 38, 43–47, 71–74, 83–85. *STC* 22685.

Smith, Sir Thomas. *De republica Anglorum.* 1583. Wife's obedience, Bk. I, Chap. 11; a woman's inability to govern, Chap. 16. *STC* 22857.

Stubbes, Philip. *The Anatomie of Abuses.* 1583. *STC* 23376.

Wilkinson, Robert. *The Merchant Royall. A Sermon.* 1607. Silence and obedience of the wife, 8, 18, 37–38. *STC* 25657.

CHAPTER TWO: Limitations by Law and Custom

Ascham, Roger. *The Scholemaster*, ed. Edw. Arber. London, 1870. Punishments given Lady Jane Grey by parents, 47.
Bateson, Mary. *Borough Customs*. London, 1906. Selden Society, vol. 21. Coming of age, II, p. cxxvii.
Beaven, A. B. *The Aldermen of the City of London*. London, 1908, 1913. Wells and Irlond, II, 6, 12, and Index.
Brinkelow, Henry. *The co-Plaint of Roderyck Mors for the Redresse of Certeyn Wyked Lawes*. 1548 (?). An early attack on arranged marriages. *STC* 3760.
Calendar of State Papers, Dom. Ser. London, 1856. Wardship of daughters held by Lady Elizabeth Russell, I, 432.
Campbell, Mildred. *The English Yeoman under Elizabeth and Early Stuarts*. New Haven, London, 1942. Arranged marriages, 283–284, also Chap. VII.
Chamberleyne, Edw. *Angliae notitia, or the Present State of England*. London, 1702. 20th ed. Inherited titles of women and kings' gifts of titles to women, 308–310.
Cleaver, Robt. *A Godly Form of Householde Government*. 1598. Important ideas, 112–116, 221. *STC* 5382.
Cogan, Thomas. *The Haven of Health*. 1584. General background. *STC* 5478.
Davey, R. P. B. *The Nine Days' Queen*. London, 1909. Beating of Lady Jane Grey by mother, 230–231.
Dictionary of National Biography. Lady Mary Cholmondeley and other minor people.
E., T. *The Lawes Resolutions of Womens Rights*. 1632. Legal restrictions on women, Bk. I, sec. iii, etc. *STC* 7437.
Finch, Mary E. *The Wealth of Five Northamptonshire Families*. Oxford, 1955. Northamptonshire Record Society, vol. 19. For general background see Preface by H. F. Habbakuk, also Chap. III.
Gairdner, Jas. (ed.) *The Paston Letters*. London, 1904. Elizabeth Paston and Scrope, II, Nos. 93–94: Margery and Richard Calle, V, Nos. 710, 713, 721.
Gilbert, Davies. *The Parochial History of Cornwall*. London, 1838. Thomasine Bonaventura, IV, 132–135.
Harrison, Wm. *The Description of England*, ed. Georges Edelen. Ithaca, 1968. Titles held by women, 103.
Holdsworth, Wm. *A History of English Law*. London, 1942 (rpt., 1966). Vol. III, wardship and marriage, 61–66; inheritance, 171–175; tenancy by the curtesy, 185–189; dower, 189–197; coming of age, 510; the married woman, 520–527; chattels and real chattels, 526–527.
Letters and Papers of . . . Henry VIII. London, 1862–1910. Wardship and marriage of young Duke of Suffolk held by his mother, XXI, Pt. I, No. 963 (2).
Littleton, Sir Thomas. *Tenures*. Norman-French editions, 1489–1639. *STC* 15719–15759. English editions. 1525?–1630. *STC* 15760–15789.
Noye, Wm. *A Treatise of the Principall Grounds and Maximes of the Lawes of This Kingdome*. London, 1641. The six ages of a woman, 47.
Paynell, Thomas. *Regimen sanitatis Salerni*. 1528. General background. *STC* 21596.
Pollock, Sir Frederic and F. M. Maitland. *The History of English Law before the Time of Edw. I*. Cambridge, 1911. Vol. I, women in private and public law, 482–485. Vol. II, the doctrine of impartible succession, 262–264; definition of dower, 404; tenancy by the curtesy, 414–418; ownership of chattels, 427; wills made by married women, 428.
Read, Evelyn. *Catherine, Duchess of Suffolk*. London, 1962. Attempts of Sir Christopher Willoughby to claim niece's property as the male heir, 24–25, 170.
Sayles, G. O. *Select Cases in the Court of King's Bench under Edward I*. Vol. III. London, 1939 (rpt., 1972). Selden Society, vol. 58. Use of marriage settlement in liturgy, 54–56.
Sheehan, Michael M. "The Influence of Canon Law on the Property Rights of Married Women in England," *Mediaeval Studies*, XXV (1963), 109–124. Endowment of bride part of the liturgy, 114; use of moral pressure for wife's property rights, 116; efforts to establish a wife's right to own chattels and make a will, 122–124.

Statutes of the Realm, ed. A. Luders, T. E. Tomlins, J. Raithby, *et al.* London, 1810–1828. Dower, IV, Pt. I, 404. For other details, see volume for the year named and index for topic.

Stockwood, John. *A Bartholomew Fairing for Parentes.* 1589. *STC* 23277.

Stone, Lawrence. *The Crisis of the Aristocracy, 1558–1641.* Oxford, 1965. Wills limiting marriage of daughters, 595; wardships, 600–605, 652, 739; marriage of son and heir, 632; portions, 636–640; few able-bodied girls in nunneries even before the Dissolution, 646–647; examples of early marriages, 657.

Swinburne, Henry. *A Treatise of Spousels or Matrimonial Contracts.* London, 1686. General background.

Thompson, Craig R. (ed.) *The Colloquies of Erasmus.* Chicago, London, 1965. Duty of mothers to suckle their own children, 272–273.

Thrupp, Sylvia L. *The Merchant Class of Mediaeval London, 1300–1500.* Chicago, Toronto, London, 1948. Advancement by marriage, 106–178; profit of Wells and Irlond, 106–107.

Tregellas, Walter H. *Cornish Worthies.* London, 1884. Thomasine Bonaventura, I, 151–157.

Tusser, Thomas. *Five Hundreth Pointes of Good Husbandrie . . . with Huswiferie.* 1573. Duty of mothers to suckle their children, fol. 78. *STC* 24375.

Whetstone, Geo. *An Heptameron of Civill Discourses.* 1582. "The Second Dayes Exercise." *STC* 25337.

Wilkins, Geo. *The Miseries of Enforced Marriage.* Oxford, 1964. Malone Society Reprints. For factual source of play, Intro., vi-vii.

Williams, Ethel Carleton. *Bess of Hardwick.* London, New York, 1959. Financial gains of Bess by marriages, 7, 10–11, 40–41, 197–198.

Williamson, Geo. C. *Lady Anne Clifford,* Kendal, 1922. Efforts by law to recover her father's property, Chap. V; Chap. X, 172–173; Chap. XI.

MANUSCRIPT MATERIAL FROM PUBLIC RECORD OFFICE, LONDON

PRO 29/154, 29/1045. Court of King's Bench. Trial of Agnes Hungerford for murder.

PRO C/199/63. Petition in Chancery of Richard Elyot and his wife.

Prerogative Court of Canterbury Wills (once at Somerset House, now at PRO)

1503. Percival, Sir John. St. Mary Woolnoth, London. Cheshire. 23 Blamyr.

1513. Percival, Dame Thomasyn (formerly Gall and Barnaby). St. Mary Woolnoth, London. St. Mary Wyke, Cornwall. 28 Fetiplace.

1521. Hungerford, Sir Edw. Heytesbury, Wilts. 21 Maynwaryng.

1565. Saint Lo, Sentlowe, Sir Wm., knt. Chatsworth, Derby. With sentence, 24 Morrison.

1590. Shrewsbury, Earl of, Geo. Sheffield, Yorks. Notts. 86 Drury.

CHAPTER THREE: Women Officeholders

Callis, Robt. *The Reading . . . upon the Statute . . . of Sewers.* London, 1647. Lecture "quarta," stating that Margaret was put in the commission, 199–201.

Clark, Alice. *Working Life of Women in the Seventeenth Century.* London, 1919 (rpt., 1968). Women as executors of wills, 39.

Collins, Arthur. *Letters and Memorials of State.* London, 1746. Sir Philip Sidney's will, I, 112.

Cox, J. O. *Churchwardens' Accounts.* London, 1913. Women wardens, 7; duties, Chap. II.

Gasquet, F. A. *Parish Life in Mediaeval England.* London, 1906. Women wardens, 106; duties, 103–107, 108–112, 132–136, 237–246.

Letters and Papers of . . . Henry VIII. Petition of Lord Darcy, XII, Pt. 2, No. 186 (35).

Lists of Sheriffs. London, 1908. Vol. IX, Lists and Indexes, PRO. See individual name and date.

Noye, Wm. See Rachel R. Reid, 87–91.

Pollock, Sir Frederic and F. M. Maitland. *The History of English Law before the*

Time of Edward I. Cambridge, 1898. Vol. I, rights of women, 482–485; husbands of peeresses in Parliament, 483. Vol. II, 262, 437–438.

Putnam, Bertha Haven. *Early Treatises on the Practice of the Justices of the Peace in the Fifteenth and Sixteenth Centuries.* Oxford, 1924. Oxford Studies in Social and Legal History, vol. 7. Comments of lawyers on women in unusual positions, 194–195; some examples, 196, footnote 1; 197; 310, note 3; Appendix III, 310.

Reid, Rachel R. *The King's Council in the North.* London, New York, 1921. Margaret Beaufort and other women in unusual positions, 87–91; also Appendix 486–487.

Sheehan, Michael M. "The Influence of Canon Law on the Property Rights of Married Women in England," *Mediaeval Studies,* XXV (1963), 109–124. Unsuccessful efforts of canonists to establish a wife's right to chattels and making a will, 122–124.

Statutes of the Realm, ed. A. Luders, T. E. Tomlins, J. Raithby. London, 1810–1828. See volume for reign of Henry VIII and the year named.

Williamson, Geo. C. *Lady Anne Clifford.* Kendal, 1922. Isabella de Clifford, 394: Lady Anne Clifford as sheriff, Chap. XXIV.

WILLS

A Collection of Lancashire and Cheshire Wills, 1301–1752, ed. W. F. Irvine. Lincoln's Inn Fields, 1896.

English Wills, 1498–1526, ed. A. F. Cirket. Streatley near Luton, Beds., 1957. Beds. Hist. Record Society, vol. 37.

Hall, E. Vine. *Testamentary Papers: Wills from Shakespeare's Town and Time.* London, 1933, 2 vols. All analyzed for women as executors.

Nicolas, N. H. *Testamenta vetusta.* London, 1826. Will of Henry VII, 26; John Lord Berners, 328; Henry Colet, 481; John Colet, 568.

Tudor Church Music, ed. Buck, Fellowes, *et al.* London, 1922–1929. Will of Tallis, VI, xxi.

Wills from Doctors Commons, ed. Nichols and Bruce. Camden Society, vol. 83 (1863). Chas. Brandon, 29; Sir Thomas Gresham, 57; Sir Francis Walsingham, 69.

Wills and Inventories . . . of the Northern Counties of England. London, 1835. Surtees Society, vol. 2.

Wills and Inventories from the Registers of . . . Bury St. Edmunds, ed. Samuel Tymms. Camden Society, vol. 49 (1850).

MANUSCRIPT MATERIAL

PCC 1564. Anne Walsingham, wife of F. Walsingham, esq. Parksbury, Herts. 32 Stevenson.

CHAPTER FOUR: Women in Business: Large Affairs

Abrams, Annie. *Social England in the Fifteenth Century.* London, New York, 1909. Margery Russell, Margaret Cokkes, 136–137; others, Chap. V.

Bateson, Mary. *Borough Customs.* London, 1904. Selden Society, vol. 18. Married and single women as traders, I, 227–228; female apprentices, 229–230.

Calendar of Letter-Books . . . of the City of London, ed. R. B. Sharpe. London, 1899–1912. Vols. A through L. See index for names of women.

Chancery. *List of Early Chancery Proceedings in the PRO.* Vols. I–III. London, 1901, 1903, 1906. (Vols. XII, XVI, XX in Lists and Indexes.) Russell and Pafford, 6/120, 6/247; others as feme sole, 64/607, 64/883, 110/125, 201/32.

Clark, Alice. *Working Life of Women in the Seventeenth Century.* London, 1919 (rpt., 1968). Joan Dant, 32–33; other women capitalists, 25–31.

Holdsworth, Sir Wm. *A History of English Law.* London, 1942 (rpt., 1966). Queens granted right to operate as if feme sole, III, 525.

Pepys, Samuel. *Diary,* ed. Latham and Matthews. Berkeley, Los Angeles, 1970. Items on Mrs. Bland, in 1662, III, 300; in 1664, V, 265–266.

Waters, Charlotte M. *An Economic History of England,* 1066–1874. London, 1925 (rpt., 1961). Women in business, Pts. III, IV.
Winchester, Barbara. *Tudor Family Portrait.* London. 1955. Jane Rawe, 84; Mrs. Fayrey, 84–85; Mrs. Margaret Baynham, 85, 131–135, 252.

MANUSCRIPT MATERIAL

Corydon, Margaret: in business as a feme sole *ex assensu viri* in the latter part of the reign of Henry VIII. London City Repertories, IX, fol. 398. (Item furnished me by Marjorie Gesner, Dept. of History, Michigan State University.)

CHAPTER FIVE: Women in Business, Gild Members: Small Affairs

Black Book of Southampton, ed. A. B. W. Chapman. Southampton, 1912. Southampton Record Society, vol. 13. Women woolpackers, I, xxxi.
Calendar of Letter-Books . . . of the City of London, ed. R. B. Sharpe. London, 1899–1912. See names of women in indexes.
Calendar of State Papers, Dom. Ser . . . Chas. I. London, 1860. Grant of arms to silk throwers, IV, 28; petition in 1630 of silkmen, 390.
Clark, Alice. *Working Life of Women in the Seventeenth Century.* London, 1919 (rpt., 1968). Organization of industry, 6–8; complaint of weavers, 103; lists of tradeswomen in Oxford and Yorkshire, 155.
Coventry Leet Book, ed. Maud Dormer Harris. EETS, 134 (1907). Women in business, I, Intro., xxviii, xli, and Notes; also 545, 568.
Dale, Marian K. "The London Silkwomen of the Fifteenth Century," *Economic History Review,* IV (1932–1934), 324–355.
Dixon, E. "Craftswomen in the Livre des Métiers," *Economic Journal,* V (1895), 209–228.
Green, Mrs. J. R. *Town Life in the Fifteenth Century.* New York, London, 1894. Married women as merchants, and ways for a woman to become a gild member in Totnes, II, 33.
Harrison, Wm. *The Description of England,* ed. F. J. Furnivall. London, 1887–1891. Increase in number of silkshops and change to management by men.
Heaton, Herbert. *The Yorkshire Woollen and Worsted Industries.* Oxford, 1920. Oxford Hist. and Lit. Studies, vol. 10. Women in wool industry, 23, 38, 93, 110, 345.
Herbert, Wm. *The History of the Twelve Great Livery Companies of London.* London, 1836, 1837. Vol. I, women in Brewers Co., 62, 63, 84, and notes; in Grocers Co., 83–84, 306; in Drapers Co., 423 and notes 444, 466; in Fishmongers Co., 68, also II, 21, 44; Taylors & Linen Armourers Co., II, 383, 385, 413.
Hill, Christopher. "Puritans and the Poor," *Past and Present,* No. 2 (November, 1952), 32–50. Changes in attitude.
Hollingsworth, T. H. *Historical Demography.* London, 1969. Population growth, 387.
Leet Jurisdiction in the City of Norwich, ed. Wm. Hudson. London, 1892. Selden Society, vol. 5. Women selling without being citizens or breaking other rules, 55, 57, 60, 63, 72, 91. (One fine listed is as late as 1555.)
Lipson, Ephraim. *The Economic History of England.* 12th ed., 1959 (rpt., 1966). Women in early industry, I, 359–363; development of problems with capitalism, 471–475; Jack of Newbury and other weavers, 475–479.
———. *The History of the Woollen and Worsted Industries.* London, 1921. General background, Chaps. I, II. Winchcombe and other weavers, 45–52; women workers, 62–66.
Pecock, Reginald. *The Reule of Chrysten Religioun.* EETS, 171 (1927). Help of wives in support of family, 320–321.
Ricart, Robert. *The Maire of Bristow Is Kalendar,* ed. Lucy T. Smith. Camden Society, vol. 5 (1872). Apprentices of the wife in family, 103.
Rich, E. E. "The Population of Elizabethan England," *Economic History Review,*

sec. ser., II, No. 3 (1950), 247–265. Difficulty of estimating populations, aliens, 263.
Russell, J. C. *Late Ancient and Mediaeval Population.* Philadelphia, 1958. Changes in populations, 118–119.
Sellers, Maud. "The City of York in the Sixteenth Century," *English History Review,* IX (1894), 275–304. General background.
————. *York Memorandum Book.* Durham, London, Berlin, 1912. Surtees Society, vol. 120. Women in trades and crafts, xxviii–xxix, l, lv; also 6, 8, 9, 10–12, 82, 114, 180.
Smith, Toulmin. *English Gilds,* with Intro. by Lucy T. Smith, EETS, 40 (1870). Women in gilds, Intro., xxx; also 16, 17–18, 46, 47, 71–73, 107, 155, 160, 169, 172–175.
Stationers Company
    Arber, Edw. *A List Based on the Registers of the Stationers Company of 837 London Publishers . . . 1553–1640.* Birmingham, 1890.
    Greg, W. W. and E. Boswell. *Records of the Court of the Stationers Company, 1576–1602.* London, 1930.
    Jackson, Wm. A. *Records of the Court of the Stationers Company, 1602–1640.* London, 1957. Relief for widows, 22–24; transfer of right to Raleigh's *History,* 152; fines for breaking rules, 259, 480; fee for leave to print book, 489.
Statutes of the Realm, ed. A. Luders, T. E. Tomlins, J. Raithby, *et al.* London, 1810–1828. Act for bringing organizations under control of the king, III, 37 Henry VIII, c. 4. See III, IV, Indexes, for other items on control of gilds. See act requiring labor from those with income below a certain amount, IV, 5 Eliz., c. 4; act voiding contracts for interest above 10%, IV, 13 Eliz. (1571), c. 8.
Stone, Lawrence. *The Crisis of the Aristocracy, 1558–1641.* Oxford, 1965. Interest on money, 529–530.
Thompson, Craig R. (ed.). *The Colloquies of Erasmus.* Chicago, London, 1965. Mother's duty to nurse her child, 272–273.
Thrupp, Sylvia L. *The Merchant Class of Mediaeval London, 1300–1500.* Chicago, 1948. Women in industry, their education, their apprenticeship, 169–174.
Tucker, G. S. L. "English Pre-Industrial Population Trends." *Economic History Review,* sec. ser., XVI, No. 2 (1963), 205–218. Important details, 210–211.
Unwin, George. *Studies in Economic History: The Collected Papers of George Unwin,* ed. R. H. Tawney. London, 1927 (rpt., 1958). See "Mediaeval Gilds and Education," pp. 92–99.
Victoria Hist. of the Co. of Berkshire. London, 1923. Women traders, III, 533.
Waters, Charlotte M. *An Economic History of England, 1066–1874.* London, 1925 (rpt., 1961). Facts about women, 17–18, 46–47, 73, 107, 169, 170–173, 205–207.
Young, Sidney. *The Annals of the Barber-Surgeons of London.* London, 1890. Facts about women, 252–253, 260; Appendix A.

CHAPTER SIX: Women as Manor Wives or in Other Large Households

Brook, V. F. K. *A Life of Archbishop Parker.* Oxford, 1962. Details about Margaret Parker, 36–37, 254–255.
Complete Peerage, ed. Vicary Gibbs, *et al.* London, 1910–1959.
Cooper, Wm. D. "The Expenses of the Judges of Assize . . . 1598–1601," *Camden Miscellany,* IV, Camden Society, vol. 73 (1858). Intro. and 15–43.
Cross, Claire. *The Puritan Earl: The Life of Henry Hastings . . . Earl of Huntingdon.* London, Melbourne, Toronto, New York, 1966. Margaret Dakins Hoby, 24, 56–58, 172.
Ducarel, Andrew. *The History . . . of the Archepiscopal Palace of Lambeth.* London, 1785. Palace rooms, 40–44; rules for officers serving Margaret Parker, Appendix VIII, 29–39.

Emmison, F. G. *Tudor Secretary: Sir William Petre at Court and Home.* London, 1961. Details of life, 131–132, 240–243.

———. *Tudor Food and Pastimes.* London, 1964. Details in Chap. II.

Fox, Evelyn. "The Diary of an Elizabethan Gentlewoman," *Trans. of the Royal Hist. Society,* 3rd ser., II (1908), 153–174. Religious activities of Margaret Dakins Hoby, 160; her belief in illness as punishment for sin, 161; her care for the sick and the injured, 162; her activities, 164–166; her amusements, 167.

Gairdner, Jas. (ed.) *The Paston Letters.* London, 1904. Margaret Paston's ejection from Gresham, II, Nos. 103, 127, 182, 184; her struggle over Drayton, IV, Nos. 578–579, 581–585, 599, 609.

Harley. *Letters of the Lady Brilliana Harley,* ed. T. T. Lewis. Camden Society, vol. 58 (1853). See 13–14, 24, 34, 40, 42, 46, 78–80, 140, 178, 188, 198, 202, 205.

Harrison, Wm. *The Description of England,* ed. Georges Edelen. Ithaca, 1968. Making beer for a household, 137–138.

Hoby, Margaret. *Diary,* ed. Dorothy M. Meads. Boston, New York, 1930. Marriages, 5–12, 24, 32; unwelcome guests, 40–43; details of daily life, 46–48, 62–72; her dressing wounds, 100, 101, 110.

Holdsworth, Sir Wm. *A History of English Law.* London, 1956 (rpt., 1966). Duties of justices of the peace, I, 285–298.

Lambarde, Wm. *Eirenarcha.* 1581. STC 15163. Increasing duties and small pay of justices of the peace, Bk. i, c. 7; Bk. iv, c. 21.

Letters and Papers . . . of Henry VIII. London, 1862–1910. In volume for year named, see Index.

Nichols, John. *The Progresses and Public Processions of Queen Elizabeth.* London. 1823. The entertainments given by the Parkers, I, 201, 325, 331–332, 340–347.

Notestein, Wallace. *English Folk.* London, Toronto, 1938. Lady Harley, 278–308.

Parker, Matthew. *Correspondence.* Cambridge, 1853. Parker Society, vol. 33. Queen's attitude to wife of a clergyman, 148, 156; queen's grant for 40 servants, 175; other details, 190, 368–369.

Perry, Edith Weir. *Under Four Tudors.* London, 1949 (rpt., 1964). Entertainment by Parkers at Old Palace, Canterbury, 250–253.

Pickthorn, Kenneth. *Early Tudor Government: Henry VII.* Cambridge, 1934 (rpt., New York, 1967). Duties of landed gentry and others on commissions, Chap. 3.

———. *Early Tudor Government: Henry VIII.* Cambridge, 1934. Members of Council on commissions of the peace, 21.

Plumpton Correspondence, ed. Thomas Stapleton. Camden Society, vol. 4 (1839). Letters, cx, 170, 171, 184, 186, 188; letter from Isabel to husband, 198.

Read, Conyers (ed.). *William Lambarde and Local Government.* Ithaca, 1962. Methods of work by justices of the peace, "An Ephemeris," 15–52.

Smyth, John. *The Berkeley MSS: The Lives of the Berkeleys,* ed. Sir John Maclean. Gloucester, 1883. Vol. II, letter of Isabel to husband, 62–63; her imprisonment and death, 70, 80, 81.

Stone, Lawrence. *The Crisis of the Aristocracy, 1558–1641.* Oxford, 1965. Facts on childbirth, 167–174, 589–592.

Tusser, Thomas. *Five Hundreth Pointes of Good Husbandrie . . . with Huswiferie.* 1573. STC 24376.

Walter of Henley's Husbandry . . . Anonymous Husbandry, Seneschaucie, Robert Grosseteste's Rules, ed. Elizabeth Lamond. London, 1890. Intro., xl–xliv; Grosseteste's *Rules,* 122–145.

Weigall, Rachel. "An Elizabethan Gentlewoman," *QR,* No. 428 (July, 1911), 119–138. Account of Grace Sherrington, Lady Mildmay: her mother's beating her, 119–120; her education, 120–121; her daily activities, 125; her charities, 129; her care of the sick, 130–133.

Winchester, Barbara. *Tudor Family Portrait.* London, 1955. Sabine Johnson as manor wife, Chap. 4; duties of Sabine, 94–95; her accounts and accountant, 96 and Index; her children, 100–102.

CHAPTER SEVEN: Women, from Royalty to Common Folk, in Various
Activities

Acts of the Privy Council, ed. J. R. Dasent. London, 1890–1907. Refusal of Coun-
cil to stop Dering's lectures, VIII, 120, 133.
Bonaventura [Percival], Thomasine.
    Carew of Antony, Richard. *The Survey of Cornwall*, ed. F. E. Halliday. Lon-
      don, 1953. See 187–188.
    Gilbert, Davies. *The Parochial History of Cornwall*. London, 1838. IV, 131–
      135.
    Tregellas, Walter H. *Cornish Worthies*. London, 1884. I, 151–157.
Calendar of the Patent Rolls, Eliz., 1558–1560. London, 1939. Grant to Lavina Ter-
    ling, I, 41.
Clitherow, Margaret
    Biographical Dictionary of English Catholics. London, New York, 1885–1902.
      I, 517.
    Dictionary of National Biography.
    New Catholic Encyclopedia. 1967. III, 959.
Collins, Arthur. *Letters and Memorials of State*. London, 1746. Will of Anne,
    Countess of Warwick; almshouse, I, 43.
Collinson, Patrick. *A Mirror of Elizabethan Puritanism*. London, 1964. Details on
    Dering, 4, 5, 12, 15–18, 23, 28.
———. *The Elizabethan Puritan Movement*. Berkeley, Los Angeles, 1967. Edw.
    Dering, 118, 135, 360, 434, 435.
———. "The Role of Women in the English Reformation. Illustrated by the Life
    and Friendships of Anne Locke." See *Studies in Church History*, ed. G. J.
    Cuming. London, 1965. Article by Collinson, 258–272.
Conway, Wm. *The Writings of Albrecht Dürer*. New York, 1956. Comment on
    Hornebolt, 120.
Coverdale, Miles. *Remains*. Cambridge, 1846. Parker Society, vol. 14. Life, vii–xvi;
    his letter to Parker on his finances, 529.
Croft-Murray, Edw. *Decorative Painting in England*. London, 1962. Carmillion,
    1, 17, 157–158.
Dering, Edw. *Maister Derings Workes*. 1614. Letters to religious women. *STC* 6678.
    Also *STC* 6676, 6677.
Dictionary of National Biography. For Bonaventura, Clitherow, Inglis, Hornebolt,
    Jane Shore, and others.
Dunkel, Wilbur. *William Lambarde, Elizabethan Jurist*. New Brunswick, 1965.
    College of the Poor, 49–54.
Ellis, Sir Henry. *Original Letters*. London, 1827. 2nd ser. Otwell Johnson on the
    racking of Anne Askew, II, 177.
Faulkner, Thomas. *An Historical . . . Description of Chelsea*, Chelsea, 1829. Anne
    Fiennes, I, 231–232; Emmanuel Hospital, II, 104–105.
Field, Nathaniel. *Amends for Ladies*. 1639. Picture of Mary Frith. *STC* 10853.
Foxe, John. *Acts and Monuments*, ed. Josiah Pratt. London, 1877. Askew, V, 537–
    550.
Haydn, Jos. *Book of Dignities*. London, 1894. List of bishoprics, for Coverdale, 424.
Inglis, Esther. MSS Books, F. S. L: V.a, 91, 92, 93, 94.
Jackson, Dorothy J. *Esther Inglis, Calligrapher*. New York, 1937. Chief source of
    facts used here. Mrs. Jackson is preparing a revision of her book.
Jordan, W. K. *The Development of Religious Toleration in England*. Cambridge,
    Mass., 1932. Important ideas, 28–30, 38, 89–90, 96–97.
———. *Philanthropy in England, 1480–1660*. London, 1959. Important ideas, 17,
    45, 156–165, 179, 221–222, 269, 274, 353–355; also Tables, 382–383.
Kendall, Paul M. *The Yorkist Age*. Garden City, N.Y., 1965. Agnes Forster, 402–
    404.
Klein, A. J. *Intolerance in the Reign of Elizabeth, Queen of England*. Boston, 1917.
    Important ideas, 58–59, 70, 83, 89–90, 96–97.
Letters and Papers . . . of Henry VIII. London, 1862–1910. See volume for date
    given and Index for name of artist.
Locke, Anne [or Prowse, name by last marriage]. Translations from the French:
    Calvin, John. *Sermons upon the Songe that Ezechias Made*. 1560. *STC* 4450.

Taffin, Jean. *Of the Markes of the Children of God.* 1590. *STC* 23652.

Machyn, Henry. *Diary,* ed. J. G. Nichols. Camden Society, vol. 42 (1848). Wife of Thomas Arden, vol. 4, and note on 315.

Maidment, Jas. *Analecta Scotica.* Edinburgh, 1834. Letter from Esther Inglis to James I, asking help for her son to study theology, I, Letter XXXVI.

Meadows, Denis. *Elizabethan Quintet.* London, New York, Toronto, 1956. Popular life of Mary Frith, 238–263.

More, St. Thomas. *The History of King Richard III.* New Haven, London, 1963. *The Complete Works,* vol. 2. Account of Jane Shore, 54–56.

Mozley, John F. *John Foxe and his Book.* London, New York, 1940. Foxe in household of the Duchess of Suffolk, 30, 48.

Mullinger, Jas. Bass. *The University of Cambridge . . . to 1535.* Cambridge, 1873. Founding of Clare College, 250–252.

Nelson, Wm. *John Skelton, Laureate.* New York, 1939. Pietro Carmeliano and Ellys Carmylyon, 4–19.

Nichols, John. *The Progresses . . . of Queen Elizabeth.* London, 1823. Lavina Terling and New Year's gifts, I, 117, 126.

Nichols, John Gough. "Notices of the Contemporaries and Successors of Holbein," *Archaeologia,* XXXIX, Pt. I (1863). His view on Carmylyon, 39, 19–46.

Percival. See Bonaventura, Thomasine.

Pollard, A. F. *The History of England, from the Accession of Edward VI to the Death of Elizabeth.* London, New York, 1910. Number of heretics executed under Mary and under Elizabeth, 376–377.

Reynolds, Graham. *English Portrait Miniatures.* London, 1952. General background and also 7.

Ridley, Jasper. *Thomas Cranmer.* Oxford, 1962. Refusal of Lieutenant of Tower to rack Anne Askew, 254.

Ringler, Wm., Jr. *The Poems of Sir Philip Sidney.* Oxford, 1962. Details about Penelope Rich, 435–443.

Shore, Jane. *The Life and Character of. . . .* London, 1714. Anonymous brief life, about 20 pages.

Stone, Lawrence. *The Crisis of the Aristocracy, 1558–1641.* Oxford, 1965. Social responsibility assumed by aristocrats, 49; Puritan support, both men and women, 733–739.

Stow, John. *A Survey of London,* ed. C. L. Kingsford. Oxford, 1908. Women philanthropists, I, 116; Christ's Hospital, 319.

Trevelyan Papers, ed. J. Payne Collier. Camden Society, 67 (1857). Payments to Lavina Terling, 195, 203, 205. Camden Society, vol. 84 (1863). Other payments, 18, 25, 31.

Wilenski, R. H. *Flemish Painters.* New York, 1960. Susanna Hornebolt, I, 105, 106, 130; L. Teerlinck, 130, 152, 175.

Williamson, Geo., and Percy Buckman. *The Art of the Miniature Painter.* London, 1926. Terling and Hornebolt, 12–13.

Williamson, Geo. C. *Lady Anne Clifford,* Kendal, 1922. Almshouses, Chap. XXII.

Wriothesley, Chas. *A Chronicle of England . . . 1495–1559.* Camden Society, vol. 11 (1875–1877). Anne Askew, 155, 167, 169.

MANUSCRIPT MATERIAL

PRO. Court of King's Bench, 29/154, 29/1045. Trial of Agnes Hungerford for the murder of her first husband.

Prerogative Court of Canterbury wills (once at Somerset House, now in PRO). 1503. Percival, Sir John. St. Mary Woolnoth, London. Cheshire. 23 Blamyr. 1513. Percival (formerly Gall and Barnaby), Dame Thomasyn. St. Mary Woolnoth, London. St. Mary Wyke, Cornwall. 28 Fetiplace.

CHAPTER EIGHT: Women with a Sound Classical Education

Armitage-Smith, Sidney. *John of Gaunt.* Westminster, 1904 (rpt., New York, 1964). Catherine Swynford and the Beauforts, Table V, 389, 390–391.

Ascham, Roger. *The Scholemaster,* ed. Edw. Arber. London, 1870. Talk with Lady Jane Grey about her education, 46–48.

————. *The Whole Works,* ed. J. A. Giles. London, 1865. Letter to Sturm about Mildred Cecil's ability to speak Greek, I, Pt. I, lxx–lxxi; to Mary Roper, lxxxiv; to Doctor Cole, I, Pt. II, No. 187.

Baker, Thomas. *History of the College of St. John the Evangelist,* ed. J. E. B. Mayor. Cambridge, 1869. Pay to Greek and Hebrew lecturers, I, 100.

Ballard, Geo. *Memoirs of British Ladies.* London, 1775. Sketches of many women, with useful sources. See Index.

Barker [Bercher], Wm. *The Nobility of Women,* ed. R. Warwick Bond. London, 1904. Important details, 151–154.

Bennett, H. S. *Six Medieval Men and Women.* Cambridge, 1955. Margery Kempe, 124–150.

Berners, Dame Juliana (?). *The Book of Hawking, Hunting, and Blasing of Arms.* 1486, 1496. STC 3308, 3309.

Bradner, Leicester, and Chas. A. Lynch. *The Latin Epigrams of Thomas More.* Chicago, London, 1953. Satirical epigrams, Nos. 98, 147, 149, 180, 189.

Calendar of State Papers, Spanish, 1558–1567. London, 1892. Lady Mary Sidney as the queen's intermediary on marriage, I, 95, 96, 98–100, 105, 107, 109, 112–133.

Chambers, P. Franklin. *Juliana of Norwich.* New York, 1955. Pt. I, "An Introductory Appreciation," 14–72; Anglican view of Thouless, 15.

Conley, C. H. *The First English Translators of the Classics.* New Haven, 1927. Translations before and after mid-century, 130–134.

Dictionary of National Biography. For Cole, Christopherson, writers at Wilton House (Nicholas Breton, Wm. Browne, Samuel Daniel, John Davies of Hereford, Abraham Fraunce) and other minor people.

Du Castel, Christine. *Here Begynneth the Book of Fayttes of Armes & of Chyvalrye,* trans. Caxton. 1489. STC 7269. See also edition by Byles, EETS, 189(1932); Intro., xi–xii.

Erasmus. *Opus Epistolorum,* ed. P. S. Allen. Oxford, 1922. Views on education of women, IV, No. 1233.

Gardiner, Dorothy. *English Girlhood at School.* Oxford, 1929. Marie of France, 57–61.

Harpsfield, Nicholas. *The Life and Death of Sir Thomas Moore,* ed. Elsie V. Hitchcock. EETS, 186 (1932). Mary Bassett, 83; Hist. Notes, 333–334.

Harrison, Wm. *The Description of England,* ed. Georges Edelen. Ithaca, 1968. The court of Elizabeth, 228–231.

Hoccleve, Thomas. *Hoccleve's Works: The Minor Poems,* ed. F. J. Furnivall. EETS, ex. ser., 61 (1892). Dedication to Joan Beaufort, Countess of Westmorland, indicating her interest in literature, I, 242.

Hogrefe, Pearl. *The Sir Thomas More Circle.* Urbana, 1959. Education of women, general facts and in drama, Chaps. VI, XII.

Jayne, Sears, and Francis R. Johnson. *The Lumley Library: The Catalogue of 1609.* London, 1956. Intro., 4–6; Jane Lumley and Mary Howard, Index.

Kempe, Margery. *The Book of Margery Kempe,* ed. Meech and Allen. EETS, 212 (1940). Chronological table, Intro., xlviii–li.

Lee, Sidney. *The French Renaissance in England.* Oxford, 1910. Seymour sisters 43, 129.

McConica, Jas. K. *English Humanists and Reformation Politics under Henry VIII and Edward VI.* Oxford, 1965. Plans for conversation in learned languages, 79.

Mulcaster, Richard. *Positions.* 1581. Ability of women to speak classical languages, Chap. 38. STC 18253.

Nelson, Wm. "Thomas More, Grammarian and Orator." *PMLA,* LVIII (1943), 337–352. More's skill in speaking Latin extempore.

Reynolds, E. E. *Margaret Roper.* London, 1960. Education of Mary Bassett and others in family, 126–127, 130–131.

Rickert, Edith. *Marie de France: Seven of her Lays Done into English.* London, 1901. Introduction.

Rogers, Elizabeth F. *Saint Thomas More: Selected Letters.* New Haven, London, 1961. More's theories of education, Nos. 17, 20, 22, 23, 29, 31, 32, 33, 35.

Ryan, Lawrence V. *Roger Ascham*. Stanford, London, 1963. Education of Princess Elizabeth and Lady Jane Grey, Index.

Scott, Mary A. *Elizabethan Translations from the Italian*. Boston, New York, 1916 (rpt., 1969). Few translations before 1550: "Index of Titles with Translators," xix–xxxiv.

Short-Title Catalogue (STC), ed. A. W. Pollard and G. R. Redgrave, London, 1926. See for early printed books not itemized separately.

Stapleton, Thomas. *The Life . . . of Sir Thomas More*, trans. Hallett. London, 1928. General background.

Thompson, Craig R. (ed.) *The Colloquies of Erasmus*. Chicago, London, 1965. Importance of Latin, Intro., xxvii–xxviii.

Underhill, John Garrett. *Spanish Literature in the England of the Tudors*. New York, 1899. Few translations before 1550, 375–377.

CHAPTER NINE: Women as Literary Patrons and as Writers

Astell, Mary. *A Serious Proposal to the Ladies*. London, 1694. Quotations from her work, 22, 73; her quotation from Wotton, 78.

Aubrey, John. *Aubrey's Brief Lives*, ed. O. L. Dick. London, 1949. Comparison of Wilton House to a college, 138–139.

Bald, R. C. *John Donne: A Life*. New York, Oxford, 1970. Godmother to Donne's daughter, 158; first contacts, 170–176; Lucy's position at court, 171–172; mutual attraction, 173; her poems, 175, 179; her gift of £30 to Donne, 295–297; his ordination, 495; his friendship with Magdalen Herbert Danvers, 495–496; chronology of his life, 537–546.

Bennett, H. S. *English Books & Readers, 1558–1603*. Cambridge, 1965. Books requested by patrons, 15–17, 31; unauthorized dedications, 53; dedications to queen, 53.

Beza, Theodore de. *The Psalmes of David*, trans. A. Gilby. 1580. Material available to the Sidneys. *STC* 2033.

Bridges, John. *An Hundred, Threescore, and Fiftene . . . Sermons*, trans. Bridges. 1572. Dedication to Earl of Bedford. *STC* 25013.

Browne, Wm. *The Poems*. London, 1894. "An Elegy on the Countess Dowager of Pembroke," II, 248–255. (A collected edition published in 1772 is not available.)

Byrne, Muriel St. Clare, and Gladys S. Thomson. "My Lord's Books," *RES*, VII (1931), 385–405. Library of 2nd. Earl of Bedford, book-lover and patron.

Calvin, John. *The Psalmes of David*, with J. Calvin's commentaries, trans. A. Golding. 1571. Material available to the Sidneys. *STC* 4395.

Clifford, Lady Anne. *The Diary*, with Intro. by V. Sackville-West. London, 1923. Her comments on the court of King James, 16–17.

Daniel, Samuel. *The Complete Works in Verse and Prose*, ed. A. B. Grosart. London, Aylesbury, 1885. In these five volumes, dedications are reprinted.

———. *A Panegyrike . . . to his Majestie*. 1603. Also *A Defence of Ryme*. *STC* 6259.

Davies, John, of Hereford. *Microcosmos*. Oxford, 1603. *STC* 6333.

———. *Wittes Pilgrimage*. 1605 (?). *STC* 6344.

———. *The Muses Sacrifice*. 1612. *STC* 6338.

Dee, John. *The Private Diary*. Camden Society, vol. 19 (1842). Visits of Sidney to Dee, 2, 20.

Dictionary of National Biography. Sir Walter Aston, Anne Halkett, Baron Harington of Exton, etc.

Donne, John. *The Poems*, ed. H. J. C. Grierson. New York, 1912. Index of first lines, 398–404.

Donne, John, the Younger (ed.) *Letters to Several Persons of Honour*. Letter to Goodyer on the gift of thirty pounds, 217–221.

Drayton, Michael. *The Barrons Wars in the Reigne of Edward the Second*. 1603. *STC* 7189.

Dunstan, A. C. *Examination of Two English Dramas.* Königsberg, 1908. Source and form of Lady Falkland's *Mariam,* 44–45.

Elton, Oliver. *Michael Drayton: A Critical Study.* London, 1905. Continued friendship with the countess, Chap. I, 14–23, and Chap. II.

Falkland, Viscountess (Elizabeth Carey). *The Tragedie of Mariam.* 1613. STC 4613. Or Malone Society Reprint, ed. A. C. Dunstan. Oxford, 1914.

Fullerton, Lady Georgiana. *The Life of Elizabeth, Lady Falkland, 1585–1639.* London, 1883.

Gardiner, Dorothy. *English Girlhood at School.* London, 1929. Makin and other women scholars of the 17th century, 242–246.

Goss, Chas. W. F. *Crosby Hall.* London, 1908. Lease by Countess of Pembroke, 89.

Gosse, Edmund W. *The Life and Letters of John Donne.* London, 1899. Personal relations, I, Chap. VII; poems by the countess, 217–218.

Halkett, Lady Anne. *Autobiography,* ed. John G. Nichols. Camden Society, 13 (1875). Her early education, 2–3.

Harington, Sir John. *Nugae antiquae,* ed. Henry Harington. London, 1804. Letter about the drunken behavior at the court of James I, 348–354.

Hutchinson, Lucy Apsley. *Memoirs of the Life of Colonel Hutchinson,* ed. Julius Hutchinson. New York, 1905. Education of Lucy, 16–17.

Jonson, Ben. *The Complete Poetry,* ed. Wm. B. Hunter, Jr., New York, 1965. Index of first lines, 479–486.

Judson, Alexander C. *The Life of Edmund Spenser.* Vol. 8, *The Works.* Baltimore, 1945. Three daughters of John Spenser, 1–7; also Alice, Anne, Elizabeth Spencer, Index.

Marston, John. *The Workes,* 1633. Dedication to Lady Falkland. STC 17471.

Meyer, G. D. *The Scientific Lady in England, 1650–1760.* Berkeley, Los Angeles, 1955. Duchess of Newcastle, 1–15, also Index.

Moffett, Thomas. *Nobilis,* a life of Sidney, ed. Heltzel and Hudson. San Marino, Cal., 1940. Sidney's attitude to astrology and chemistry, 75, 119.

Nichols, John. *The Progresses . . . of Queen Elizabeth.* London, 1823. "A Dialogue . . . in Praise of Astrea," III, 529–531.

P., W. *The Necessarie, Fit, and Convenient Education of a Yong Gentlewoman.* 1598. STC 3947, 7499.

Plomer, Henry R. *Wynkyn de Worde & his Contemporaries.* London, 1925. Statement about *The Fifteen Oes,* 51.

Rathmell, J. C. A. (ed.) *The Psalms of Sir Philip Sidney and the Countess of Pembroke.* Garden City, N.Y., 1963. Intro., xi–xxxii.

Ringler, Wm. A., Jr. *The Poems of Sir Philip Sidney.* Oxford, 1962. Intro., xliiii–xlviii; Commentary, 435–446.

Rosenberg, Eleanor. *Leicester: Patron of Letters.* New York, 1955. Patronage, Chap. I; works dedicated to him, Appendix.

Ryan, Lawrence V. *Roger Ascham.* Stanford, London, 1963. Queen's provision for Ascham and his sons, 234–240, 287–288.

Sheavyn, Phoebe. *The Literary Profession in the Elizabethan Age.* Manchester, 1909. Revised by J. W. Saunders, New York, 1967. Rewards for dedications, 18; dedications by Greene and Nash, 23–24.

Sidney, Sir Philip. *Astrophel and Stella.* 1591. (1st ed.) STC 22536. Film Acc. 572.3, B. M. copy, at F. S. L.

Smith, D. Nichol. "Authors and Patrons," in *Shakespeare's England,* II, 182–211. Oxford, 1917. Amount paid by printer, 182–183; changes in dedications for new editions, 205; unauthorized dedications, 206; rewards by some patrons, 210.

Spenser, Edmund. *The Poetical Works,* ed. Smith and de Selincourt. Oxford, 1932. Dedications usually reprinted in this edition with poems.

Spiers, W. L. *The Note-Book and Account Book of Nicholas Stone.* Walpole Society, vol. 7 (1919), 38–138. For the commission and the tentative resale, 47–48, 111.

Stillinger, Jack. "The Biographical Problem of Astrophel and Stella," *JEGP,* LIX (1960), 617–639.

Strigelius, Victorinus. *Part of the Harmony of King David's Harp,* trans. R. Robinson. 1582. STC 23358, 23359–23363.

Sweeper, Walter. *A Briefe Treatise.* . . . 1622. *STC* 23526. Not available.

Taylor, John. *The Needle's Excellency.* 10th ed. 1634. *STC* 23776.

Victoria Hist. of the Counties of England: Rutland. London, 1935. Sale of Exton Manor by 2nd Baron Harington, II, 129.

Vogt, Geo. McGill. "Richard Robinson's Eupolemia, 1603." *SP*, 21 (1934), 629–648.

Wiffen, J. H. *Historical Memoirs of the House of Russell.* London, 1833. Lucy Russell's influence on court masques, II, 63–123.

Williams, Franklin B., Jr. *Index of Dedications* . . . *in English Books before 1641.* London, 1962.

Williamson, Geo. C. *Lady Anne Clifford.* Kendal, 1922. Her education, 60–66.

Willson, D. Harris. *King James VI and I.* London, 1956. Attitude of James to women, especially to women of learning, 94–95, 196.

Wilson, F. P. "Some Notes on Authors and Patrons in Tudor and Stuart Times." *Jos. Quincy Adams Memorial Studies,* 553–561. Washington, D.C., 1948. Less need for patrons in the late seventeenth century, 355; usual pay for a pamphlet, 555.

Young, Frances B. *Mary Sidney, Countess of Pembroke.* London, 1912. Her translation of Petrarch, "Triumph of Death," 207–218.

INDEX

As this book contains many names, sources mentioned in the discussion are not usually indexed except for a few concerned with exact legal details; additional information appears in *Notes and Sources*. Names of women mentioned once will not usually be indexed, but see entries under Women for references to groups of them.

DATE DUE